Let's Get It On

Let's Get It On

TOUGH TALK FROM

BOXING'S TOP REF

AND NEVADA'S MOST

OUTSPOKEN JUDGE

MILLS LANE

WITH JEDWIN SMITH

CROWN PUBLISHERS, INC.

NEW YORK

Published by Crown Publishers, Inc., 201 East 50th Street, New York, New York 10022.
Member of the Crown Publishing Group.

Random House, Inc. New York, Toronto, London, Sydney, Auckland
www.randomhouse.com

CROWN and colophon are trademarks of Crown Publishers, Inc.

Printed in the United States of America

Library of Congress Cataloging-in-Publication Data

Lane, Mills (Mills B.), 1937–
Let's get it on : tough talk from boxing's top ref and Nevada's
most outspoken judge / by Mills Lane with Jedwin Smith. — 1st ed.
p.   cm.
Includes index.
1. Boxing—United States—Corrupt practices.   2. Boxing referees—
Nevada.   3. Lane, Mills (Mills B.), 1937–   .   I. Smith, Jedwin.
II. Title.
GV1136.5.L35   1998
796.83—dc21   98-14121
                                                      CIP

ISBN 0-609-60311-6

10 9 8 7 6 5 4 3 2 1

First Edition

This book is dedicated to the memory of
J O H N N Y   B E C K E R.

I've often remarked that no matter who you are or where you get, if you don't remember that a lot of folks helped you get there, you're nothing but a damned ingrate.

A lot of people helped me. Obviously, space prevents me from naming all of them, but certainly my mom and dad, who nurtured me, provided for me, and helped me develop values, deserve thanks. My lovely wife, Kaye, who has supported and encouraged my efforts, and my two darling sons, Tommy and Terry, whom I love so much, made doing this book such a pleasure. To all the people along the way with whom I came into contact who "kicked me in the ass" when I was not giving my best, I also owe a great deal, especially my drill instructor in the Marine Corps.

But Johnny Becker deserves special mention. I met Johnny in the early 1950s in Savannah, Georgia. We became great friends—

indeed, he was much like an older brother to me. He always called me "kid." He encouraged me, prodded me; he got "on my butt" about not writing a book a long time ago. Whenever I would go East to visit relatives, my first stop the day after I got settled would be his store on West Broughton Street.

A lot of people notice that I tweak my nose before each fight when I am introduced by the ring announcer. That tweak is for about five-hundred-plus people as a way to say "hello." But, when I gave the thumbs-up, that was for Johnny Becker. Johnny had cancer, and he was fighting the good fight and I wanted him to know it. We once talked on the telephone after a fight, and he asked me why I had given a thumbs-up when I had never done it before. I said, "Johnny, that was for you," and he said, "I knew it."

I will never forget Johnny, and even though he is no longer around to see it, every time I give the "thumbs-up," that is for him. So I dedicate this book to my dear friend—Johnny Becker. For him it will always be "thumbs-up."

CONTENTS

CONTENTS

Let's Get It On

Prefight Weigh-in

My name is Mills Lane and I'm a former Marine, a former collegiate boxer, a former professional prizefighter, and a former district attorney. Although I was born in Georgia and was raised on a farm in rural South Carolina, I call Reno, Nevada, home. It's a no-nonsense city in a no-nonsense state. People here are built of solid stuff—uncompromising ideals and values. Most of all, they stand tall on their own two feet without the aid of artificial props. I have no desire to live anywhere else.

My wife's name is Kaye and she's as beautiful a woman as any man deserves. For the past eighteen years she's given me nothing but happiness and joy. To top it off, we've been blessed with two darling sons, Terry and Tommy. I dearly love my wife and sons, and they love me. When you get right down to it, an honest man could ask for nothing more. In that regard I'm one lucky sonofabitch. The bottom line is I'm living heaven here on earth, and there are no three other people I'd rather spend my life with.

Right now I'm the district judge of Department 9, Washoe County, 2nd Judicial District Court, State of Nevada. I like to think of myself as an advocate of the people of my adopted state, a champion of the laws of these United States, and an unbending administrator of justice. Of course, there are those who believe I'm too tough on the criminal element. I don't lose any sleep over it. I view the law as if it were written in stone. Everyone has a choice—to do what's right or to do grievous wrong. It's that simple. I have no use for criminals; if convicted, and they deserve it, I send them away for a long time. The sentences I hand down are done so on behalf of a righteous people of a God-fearing nation.

I must be doing something right because I'm in the third year of my second six-year term. The people elected me.

One of my hobbies is refereeing professional prizefights. I've been doing this for the past thirty-four years. Over that span I've climbed into the ring almost seven hundred times, and I've refereed ninety-seven world championship fights. I have a love-hate relationship with the business, the gems of which will always be Muhammad Ali, Marvin Hagler, Ray Leonard, and Evander Holyfield. Unfortunately, predators defile these upstanding gentleman-athletes. Too often, as with the whole of society itself, evil overshadows good, and I've found myself having to take a stance between right and wrong.

2

Not too long ago, I disqualified Mike Tyson for twice biting the ears of Evander Holyfield, who at the time was the World Boxing Association heavyweight champion. Because Tyson's despicable behavior and the subsequent justice I handed down were witnessed by tens of millions of spectators on live television, I was catapulted into national prominence. Larry King invited me onto his show. Jay Leno, ESPN, and Bryant Gumbel did likewise. *Sports Illustrated,* the *New York Times, USA Today,* and *People* magazine did full-length feature articles on me. All of a sudden, after almost sixty years of taking life's punches and counterpunching as best I could, I was a damned celebrity. People were calling me a hero, which is downright ludicrous. I say this because, on that fateful night, I did only that which has always been asked of me: I did the right thing. Nothing more, nothing less.

I'm no more a hero than I am an author. Regardless, the kind folks calling the shots at Crown Publishers seem to think I've got something worth saying, something on the order of boxing as a metaphor for life. Imagine that.

I'm old, I'm bald, and I'm short not only in stature but also in patience with those unwilling to give their best effort. And I'm not talking about boxing. Life's nothing but one continual battle from start to finish. We come into it kicking, and if we've got an ounce of gumption, we go out the same damned way.

The way I look at things, you don't have to be a pug to know what it's like to get nailed, figuratively, by devastating left hooks or hard right hands. All of us, at one time or another, have been knocked on our butts by sickness, employment, and marital or family strife. But what makes some folks different from others—what separates the world champions from those who hang their heads and whimper and make excuses about how life is so unfair—is a willingness to tuck their chins and keep their hands held high while absorbing the punches, always pressing forward.

I measure an individual not by how many times he or she's been knocked down but by how many times he or she has gotten up. No small wonder, because I've been dumped on my butt more times than I care to remember.

I'm not a complicated individual. I believe in truth, justice, and, at the expense of sounding old-fashioned, the American way of attending to business. For the most part, our system works quite well. But we do have a few problems, the most pressing of which are the disintegration of the family, the ineffectiveness of the legal system, and, of course, the corruption of professional boxing. This is the theme of my book, and while I've tried not to beat you over the head with it, holding back has not been an easy task. After all, I am a fighter—a man who's reached his goals by continually hammering away while refusing to either back off or quit.

With that in mind, all I can do is relate where I came from, the road upon which I traveled, and the compass points by which I navigated. And while my life story most definitely has combative overtones—through prep school, the military, college, amateur and professional boxing, law enforcement, and the judiciary bench—I do not apologize for my ideals or my shortcomings, those societal misdemeanors of commission or omission.

After all, I'm just a country boy, a little guy long on Marine Corps values who wears his heart on his sleeve.

So, let's get it on . . .

The Saturday Night Blues

Mike Tyson moved in close to Evander Holyfield and pinned both of the champ's arms beneath his, clamping them against his ribs. I was attempting to break the clinch, reaching for Tyson's left elbow, when the improbable—the impossible—happened.

Although I had the best seat in the house, my view of the carnage that ensued was blocked. All I saw was the back of Tyson's head, and even now the picture remains somewhat blurred in my memory.

I never saw Tyson spit out his mouthpiece, but I did see his head rear back and then forward with great force. Like a steel trap snapping shut on its prey.

For a split second, it seemed as if the collective voice of all fight fans, sixteen thousand strong at the Las Vegas MGM Grand Garden Arena, was suddenly snuffed out. I blinked in disbelief, for when Evander Holyfield turned toward me, his face was compressed in agony—his eyes clamped tightly shut; his mouth wide open, an unuttered scream frozen in place.

And then Holyfield broke free of Tyson's grasp, spun around in a full circle, and leaped up into the air, his chin buried in his chest, his hands flailing wildly at his head. He acted like a man who had just been attacked by a swarm of hornets.

I took a step toward Evander, then hesitated and looked back at Tyson. I'll never forget his face. It was a stone-cold mask of loathing; his squinting eyes were glaring pinpricks of pure hatred. His hands were thrust out in front of him, waist high. It was almost as if he were strutting, admiring his handiwork. But I had no idea what Tyson's smug countenance was about.

And that's when the volume was turned back on. The roar of the crowd reached a crescendo, its screams cascading down into the ring and brushing hard against me with its intensity, slapping me out of shock.

I took another step toward Evander, but Tyson beat me to the punch, rushing past me as sweat glistened off his back, lunging toward the champion and shoving him in the back, pushing Holyfield hard into the ring ropes.

Only then was I able to pull Tyson away. Too late, of course. Too late to prevent insanity from reigning. Too late to prohibit the profession I love so dearly from being dragged any farther through the gutter. Too damned late for anything.

Professional boxing sustained grievous injury on that Saturday night of June 28, 1997. Such wounds take quite a while to heal.

∞∞∞∞∞

This fight seemed destined for disaster. Mike Tyson was surlier than ever leading up to the event, and according to media reports, promoter Don King actually had to beg Tyson to participate in a Monday press conference. From what I've read, Mike's comments were peculiar, to say the least. He bitched about media references to him being a monster. He also inferred that the media neither loved nor respected him.

"I have no friends," Tyson said, and then compounded the bizarre session by hypothesizing some sort of twisted bond with the late Sonny Liston, another convicted felon. "It may sound morbid and grim, but I pretty much identify with that life. . . . I think [Liston] wanted people to respect and love him, and that never happened."

And for good reason: Sonny Liston was a thug whose "strength" was his ability to intimidate people, which isn't saying a helluva lot. For Tyson to publicly infer a kinship to such a contemptible person defies logic. But what he said next goes way beyond the realm of sound reasoning.

"Basically, I've been taken advantage of my whole life," Tyson said. "I've been abused, I've been dehumanized, I've been humiliated, and I've been betrayed."

Bullshit. That's the sort of self-pitying crap I hear far too often in court, where the accused hides behind artificial excuses and refuses to stand up like a man and say, "I made a mistake and I'm sorry. Do whatever it is you have to do to correct the situation." Seldom does anyone ever admit his or her errors in such fashion. Instead, they hide behind a bunch of self-serving lies and half-truths. And that's when I tell them: "Listen, it's not because your mama didn't breast-feed you. It's not because your daddy screamed at you. The problem is you. And until you straighten yourself out, you're going to continue to have these difficulties."

I was at home in Reno when I read Tyson's diatribe. And even though at that time I had no connection to the upcoming fight, I couldn't help but wonder what in the hell was going through Mike's mind. I couldn't believe what he was saying, because it was so far removed from the man I thought I knew.

Over the years I've refereed several of his fights, and he always seemed in total control of his emotions. Sure, he's never been a very outspoken or articulate individual. But I'd never before heard him wallowing in self-pity. That wasn't his style. The Mike Tyson I knew was a magnificent fighter—a brawler, really. He was a no-nonsense, streetwise man who didn't have to rely on anything but his courage, strength, and skill in the ring. To me, he was a perfect gentleman. He always called me Mr. Mills, never Mills, even though I'd corrected him on it several times.

"No, sir," Mike would always say. "You're Mr. Mills. I respect you, sir."

And now . . . well, something wasn't ringing true. But it wasn't my problem. I was going to be several hundred miles away from the MGM Grand on that Saturday night. Instead of watching the fight on pay-per-view TV at home, I was going to make the leisurely drive into town and sit in on a few hands of poker at the Club Cal-Reno.

That had been the plan. But then controversy erupted on Wednesday over the selection of Mitch Halpern as the referee. Mitch had been the referee seven months earlier when Holyfield stunned the boxing world by knocking out Tyson in the eleventh round of their scheduled twelve-round bout for the WBA championship. Grabbing at straws, Tyson's people now complained that Tyson lost the title because Mitch had allowed excessive head butting by Evander—an unfounded allegation. Had this argument not been raised, I would not have been caught in the middle of professional boxing's darkest hour. If Tyson or Don King had not made such a big fuss, I would have been at home playing poker.

But that wasn't to be. On the Thursday morning before the fight a representative of the Nevada State Athletic Commission telephoned me and said they were having a meeting to settle the Halpern issue. I was told to keep my airplane reservation open, so I did. The next day I read in the newspaper that the commission voted 4–1 to reject the Tyson camp protest and keep Mitch as the referee, so I said the hell with it. Besides, it was too late to call the airlines and cancel my ticket.

Then, at six o'clock Saturday morning I got a call from the commission and was told, "Don't do anything. Things are changing here." They called back at eight and said, "Get on the plane and come down here. You've been assigned the fight."

That's the way it went down. But I'm still not convinced I know the whole of it.

My commission assigns me and I accept the assignment. I don't broker for fights. I don't ask for them. I'm happy to get them. A referee should not be involved in the politics of those assignments. If you're assigned, fine. If you're not, the heck with it. I don't get in bed with that stuff. I never have, I never will.

Regardless, in Vegas the day of the fight all I could think of was something my wife, Kaye, had told me. She said all the bizarre stuff in boxing happens on my watch because that Higher Power up there knows I can handle it. Kaye says I'm like a cat; no matter what happens I always land on my feet.

I don't know if that's true, but I have had some mighty weird shit happen to me. Yet nothing compared to the events that were to follow.

∞∞∞∞∞

One of my first duties in prefight preparation is visiting each of the fighters' dressing rooms. What I did that night was visit Evander Holyfield first. Accompanying me were Bob Miller, the governor of Nevada, and a couple of senators and other friends of his, plus Marc Ratner, executive director of the Nevada State Athletic Commission, and Luther Mack, a senior member of the Commission.

Introductions were made and then I told Evander, "Now look, we've been through this before many times. When the bell rings, I want you to stop punching and go right back to your corner. I don't want any of that extracurricular activity after the bell." I'd had a problem with that when he fought Riddick Bowe in their

1993 rematch at Caesars Palace. When the bell rang to end the fight in the twelfth round, both of them continued slugging it out. And when I stepped in to break it up, Bowe nailed me with a solid shot to the back of the head. I'm getting too old for that shit, but I didn't have to explain that to Evander. He just smiled and said he would comply with my wishes. And then we went over the WBA rules, including the three-knockdown rule being in effect, the rule on head butting, and no standing eight-count.

Then I asked if he would go along if the fight went the distance, with the age-old custom of touching gloves with Mike Tyson at the beginning of the last round. Although this ritual also takes place before the fight starts, it's not mandatory. It's always been a display of good sportsmanship, which is one of Evander's greatest qualities. Without hesitation, he said, "Yes sir."

The scenario was repeated in Tyson's locker room. Mike had his business face on, as usual. In fact, I didn't notice anything out of the ordinary. Certainly nothing to make me suspect that he was teetering on the edge of the abyss. He was grim-faced and ready to kick ass. There was nothing to suggest the self-pitying person the media had described days earlier, and I wondered if the guys and gals in the pressroom hadn't somehow gotten it wrong.

"How you doing, Mike?" I asked, and he responded as usual, "I'm fine, Mr. Mills." So I kept the conversation to a minimum and simply told him that he was a champion and knew the drill, and then I asked him if he would touch gloves with Holyfield if the fight went the distance.

"Yes sir, Mr. Mills," Tyson said. It was all yes sir and no sir. Mike was very polite, the consummate professional.

∞∞∞∞∞

The MGM Grand was electric when I finally climbed through the ring ropes. The place was packed and it seemed as if all sixteen thousand fans raised their voices at once when the two fighters made their way down their respective aisles to ringside.

There is nothing like this moment in all of sports. The electricity is so powerful that it actually makes the hair on your arms tingle. And as soon as the fighters enter the ring, dancing on their toes and firing punches through this highly charged atmosphere, your senses are bombarded with the overpowering smells of tension and combativeness. No matter how many times I've experienced this moment, it still makes my heart beat quicker.

And then there was a solemn hush as Jimmy Lennon, Jr., the ring announcer, intoned: "Ladies and gentlemen . . ."

Lennon's words were music to my ears, pumping up the adrenaline. This is what boxing is all about. The agonizing hours in the gym and the miles and miles of roadwork all boil down to this precise moment. It's nut-cutting time.

As I watched Tyson and Holyfield go through their final mental preparation in their respective corners, I couldn't help but share their excitement and anxiety. I'd been in that pressure-cooker myself many times—first as an amateur boxer in the Marines and at the University of Nevada-Reno, and then as a professional fighter. There is nothing heavier in the world of sports than the dreams a boxer carries with him into the ring. But, God help me, I love boxing. It is the discipline upon which my entire life has been built.

Once the usual introductions were made, I motioned Tyson and Holyfield to the center of the ring and immediately informed Tyson that, because he was wearing his trunks higher than normal, I wouldn't be calling a low blow if Evander nailed him in the navel. Tyson's second, Richie Giachetti, had no problem with that.

In my mind, I'd already gone over each boxer's strengths and weaknesses. At that moment, I actually thought I had a good idea of what to expect.

Tyson was the pit bull. He liked to move in on you quick, setting you up with the jab and knocking you senseless with his devastating right hand. He wasn't into any fancy crap—no dancing, no bobbing and weaving, nothing cute. He was a straight-ahead fighter who relied on intimidation. Too often I've seen the stark fear in the eyes of those who've had to face Tyson at his absolute best. When in close, he'd tuck his chin into his chest and defy you to hit the target. Because he was short and well-muscled, not to mention one helluva deadly counterpuncher, few men had ever succeeded in that endeavor.

Holyfield's style was in sharp contrast. The taller of the two, he was more of a pure boxer. He was better suited at cutting off the ring and was more nimble on his feet. He had a good jab and a decent right hand, but nothing to compare with Tyson's. Because of his incredible physical conditioning and stamina, though, Evander could stick you at any given point in the bout. And he could do this repeatedly. Holyfield's biggest asset, of course, was his ticker. He doesn't know how to quit. It's totally foreign to him. Without doubt, he has the biggest heart I've ever encountered in this business, which is why he's such a great champion.

If there was to be a problem with this confrontation, I figured it would happen on the inside. Their respective styles raised the likelihood of head-butts, but certainly nothing of an intentional nature. I knew both fighters to be made of better stuff. Still, the clash of heads was inevitable. While Tyson liked to go in with his head low, few fighters have been able to lean on him in similar fashion. Evander could and would, because he wasn't easily intimidated.

My final thought at that moment was, "This one's going to be a ball-buster."

I told Tyson and Holyfield they were fighting for the championship of the world, and I expected a tough clean fight and for them to protect themselves at all times. Out of respect for the champion, I asked, "Are there any questions from the challenger or his chief second?" Richie Giachetti said, "No." Then I asked, "Are there any questions from the champion or his chief second?" And Don Turner said, "No."

The fighters were primed. Sweat glistened on their massive chests. They were in the "stare," although Tyson looked down at the end. From a boxer's standpoint, this is the time when that invisible hand squeezes your scrotum and a high-voltage current moves from the tips of your toes to your heart and your head. There's no backing down now. There's no place to hide. It's hit or be hit. It's thirty-six minutes of the most demanding physical exertion known to mankind.

This Tyson and Holyfield knew without having to be reminded. I paused, then looked both fighters in the eye and said, "Okay, let's get it on."

The early going was just as I had anticipated. Mike tried to lean on Evander, but the champ leaned back. There was no intimidating

14

Holyfield. He gave back better than he received. While Tyson did manage to connect with one powerful shot to Evander's ribs, for the most part his power was negated. In my estimation, Holyfield won the first round. He hit Tyson with a straight right hand—*wham!* It really buckled Mike and he knew he'd been hit. Evander got the best of it on the inside, too.

The second round was a carbon copy of the first, except the action on the inside was a helluva lot more intense. Evander continued to give better than he received, and I believe that's when Tyson really started getting frustrated. He'd throw a punch and Evander would brush it off and counter—*whap!* And then Tyson clinched and there was a collision of heads. It was rough up close. So rough that Tyson received a nasty gash above his right eye from the impact. While Mike complained that the head-butt was intentional, I saw it as brutal but perfectly legal in-fighting.

When you get two fighters who aren't afraid to mix it up like that, butts and cuts happen. I did call time, however, and warned them: "I want both of you guys to knock that crap off. No more rough stuff inside."

Again, the second round went to Evander. He was the aggressor, in total control of the fight. But after that, everything went south. That's when it turned bizarre.

∞∞∞∞∞∞

Teddy Atlas, who helped train Mike Tyson under the tutelage of the late Cus D'Amato, said he knew the unexpected was going to happen. According to the *Boston Globe*'s Ron Borges, probably the best boxing writer around, Atlas phoned the day before the fight and laid out the following scenario:

"Mike's going to get himself disqualified," Atlas said. "He'll bite Holyfield. He'll butt him. He'll hit him low. He'll do something if he don't get him early with a lucky shot. I know this guy. He's got this all set up in his mind. The way out. That's the only way he can face it. That's what this is all about."

It was a cryptic and scary message. According to Atlas, Tyson was afraid. And he could not rationalize his fear without the presence of an out.

If that's the case, then Tyson should be hung up by his nuts. But I still have trouble believing it. What I think happened is this: In the first two rounds, Holyfield won and he won convincingly. But in the third round, Tyson started to come on. He was frustrated and angry. He also knew that he was bleeding like a stuck hog. And although he was nailing Evander with everything in his arsenal, Evander wasn't fazed in the least. I think Mike realized at that moment that, no matter what he did, he was going to get his butt kicked again. And that's when he snapped.

Therefore, when the opportunity to bite Evander's ear presented itself, Tyson just did it. While I do not think it was an accident, I also don't think he'd planned on doing it two rounds earlier. But that doesn't make it right.

Regardless of what you think of Tyson's problems with the law and his big talk, he had, at least to some degree, observed basic boxing protocol in the past. There is a certain discipline among fighters, a mutual understanding about what occurs when you strap on the gloves and come out to answer the bell. That protocol needs to be observed.

There are some things you just don't do, and biting somebody in a prizefight is certainly one of them. It's something you can expect on the amateur level, before a fighter has been seasoned by thousands of hours of grueling preparation. Once boxing maturity has been reached, one fighter biting another is the last thing you expect to see. Especially from someone as imposing as Mike Tyson.

∞∞∞∞∞

There were about forty seconds remaining in the third round when Tyson got Holyfield in the clinch, pinned both of the champ's arms against his sides, and took the initial bite that not only wounded Evander but disfigured boxing as well.

Because I was out of position, I did not see Tyson bite him. But what I did see will forever be seared into my consciousness. Evander reared back and clutched at his right ear as he leaped into the air and spun completely around. And that's when I saw the blood streaming from his ear. Talk about insane moments. You've got the roar of the crowd, two sweaty boxers at arm's-length away unloading skull-numbing punches that actually *zing* through the air. You've got a combined 450 pounds of pure mayhem thrashing about only inches away from you. You've got the heart-rending grunts and groans spilling from these guys as they pound on each other, firing lethal shots to the head and the ribs and the gut.

As the referee, you've got to preside over this licensed wrath while keeping a tight rein on order. That's the job—keeping up with the pounding action, slipping in and out of that specter of unmitigated furor and confusion, prying apart hundreds of pounds of frustration, rage, and fury. All this, and so much more.

In a fight of this magnitude, the referee is carrying a lot of unasked-for baggage. I'm referring to the responsibility of overseeing something like $65 million in purses for this one fight, plus hundreds of millions of dollars in future earnings for the winner. In addition, you've also got the vested interest of all fight fans—those who, in good faith, paid a grand for ringside seats or $100 for a ticket or laid down $50 to see the fight on pay-per-view television.

Professional boxing would die were it not for the loyalty of its fans worldwide. I'm well aware of that every time I step through those ring ropes, whether it be to referee a bout between two club fighters or a match between two of the most-celebrated boxers in the world. My job, simply put, is to protect the boxers' safety and make sure the rules are obeyed.

With that in mind, I was absolutely dumbfounded when Evander leaped into the air, blood spilling down upon his neck and shoulders. But I didn't have time to rationalize the moment, because all hell broke loose.

I started to rush to Evander's side, to see what was wrong, but I wasn't quick enough. Mike struck again by pushing Evander from behind. I grabbed Tyson's arm and yelled, "Okay, that's going to cost you a point." He glared at me with one of those "Who gives a shit" looks of contempt.

I turned and looked back to Evander's corner. Don Turner was shouting over and over: "He bit him on the ear, he bit him." I couldn't believe it. No, dammit, I didn't *want* to believe it. But sure enough, when I examined Evander's right ear, it was like raw meat. A chunk of it was missing.

Faced with this evidence, my first reaction was flawed. Seeing Marc Ratner standing on the ring apron, I approached him and said, "Tyson bit Holyfield on the ear. I'm going to disqualify him."

Marc said, "Mills, are you sure you want to disqualify him?" He didn't overrule me, and that's why Marc Ratner is such a great man. He gave me the chance to rethink my actions.

Marc's statement woke me up. My better judgment took control and I said to myself, "Wait a minute. It's time to get your brain in gear."

That's when I saw Flip Homansky, the ring doctor, in the center of the ring and I told him to take a look at Holyfield's ear and see how bad it was. Once Flip had examined the wound, I asked him, "Can he fight?" Flip said, "He can fight." I repeated the question and Flip again assured me that, although the wound was cosmetically bad, Holyfield could fight.

While this was going on, Tommy Brooks, Evander's assistant trainer, was screaming that Tyson should be disqualified. It was a nut house inside that ring. Pure bedlam. Everyone was screaming—the fans, the cornermen. Everyone except Evander Holyfield. He was furious, no doubt about it. And that's when he told Brooks, "Put the mouthpiece in. I'm going to knock this guy out."

I went to Tyson's corner and told Mike and Richie Giachetti that I was going to assess them a two-point deduction—one for the push and one for the bite. Richie didn't say anything. But Mike tried to lie his way out of it by yelling, "It was a punch."

My response: "That's bullshit, Mike. You bit him." And then I put my hand on his chest and pushed him back.

The contrast between the two fighters at that precise moment was remarkable. While Tyson was trying to duck the truth,

19

Holyfield was on his feet and ready to fight. He wanted a piece of Mike—he wanted to settle their differences once and for all.

Once order had been restored, I motioned both fighters into the center of the ring and, in no uncertain terms, said, "Look, this is a prizefight. Surely we can do better than this. I want you to knock this shit off and get down to business."

The bout resumed and Evander nailed Tyson with a helluva left hook. Then they mixed it up a little bit more, got into a clinch, and damned if Tyson didn't bite Holyfield again, this time on the left ear. Again, I couldn't believe what I was seeing. Evander stepped back, his left hand clutching his left ear, his face a contorted mask of pain. *How much would a hyped up fighter feel this?*

There was no remorse on Tyson's face. His hands were up, ready to step in and pound Holyfield some more. I stepped between the fighters and ordered them to return to their respective corners.

When I examined Evander's left ear, I was relieved to discover that it wasn't as bad as the previous bite. The ear wasn't torn; there were only the telltale teeth marks. Nonetheless, I'd seen enough. I went to Tyson's corner and chased him. I can still see him sitting on the stool, eyes glaring, his mouth open in disbelief. His cornermen were shouting at me, dumbfounded as I tugged on my left ear, indicating that while one bite was bad enough, two bites was the end of the search.

Admittedly, it took every ounce of willpower I could muster to mask my contempt for the obstinate, unrepentant creature that sat before me. I swallowed my anger and said, "That's it, Mike, you're outta here. You're gone, you're done."

And then the place went fucking nuts. Mike jumped up off his stool and screamed "Bullshit" and tried to storm across the ring toward Holyfield. I've never been so thankful for a security force in my life. Before I could even think about saving my own skin, cops materialized out of nowhere and moved me to safety. I don't know who pulled me out of the way, but I owe them a debt of gratitude. The only picture of that moment that remains in my mind is that of a suffocating wall of no-nonsense humanity enveloping the ring. And while it was absolutely crazy, it was also absolutely necessary because Tyson had lost it—not only his bid to regain the heavyweight championship of the world but his mind as well.

At that fractured moment, I truly believe Mike Tyson went nuts. And by doing so, he disgraced all of us boxers, professionals and amateurs alike. He disgraced every honest and hard-working trainer, cutman, manager, and promoter in the business, every boxing fan worldwide.

When Tyson twice bit Evander Holyfield's ears, then compounded the crime by attempting to storm across the ring to assault Holyfield further, he not only fed the flames that constantly attempt to devour our discipline, but also negated everything so many young men and, yes, even young women, have fought so long and so hard to protect—men and women whose livelihood, because of its unmitigated brutality, is constantly assailed by its critics. And that, by its very nature, is a damned shame.

∞∞∞∞∞∞

Because I have been blessed with the opportunity to referee ninety-seven title fights since 1971, I'm often asked what goes into the making of a champion. Once you go through the usual list of physical tools—hand and foot speed, stamina and endurance, a good jab and a solid right, a formidable chin and a hard head—what remains almost defies description. I speak of heart and soul, humility and humanity, all of which Evander Holyfield has in abundance.

In the aftermath of Mike Tyson's pathetic public display, Evander was taken to the Valley Hospital Medical Center in Vegas and underwent treatment to repair his damaged right ear. When that procedure was concluded, no one would have thought any less of him had he berated Tyson as a heartless goon. Instead, Evander refused to lower himself to the level of lesser men.

"I still love Mike," Holyfield said, defining "champion" far better with a few soft-spoken words than I could using the entire dictionary. "It's just those demons that possess him and make him do things. He needs to find a new savior."

Tyson, on the other hand, complained to the media about the second-round head-butt, as if that justified his gnawing of Evander's ears. "What am I to do? This is my career," Mike said. "I have children to raise. I have to retaliate."

Those are the words of a man deprived of any sensibility.

Given an opportunity to relive the final seconds of that third round and his less-than-honorable behavior afterward, I'd like to believe that Mike Tyson would react differently. Of course, that's my heart speaking. I look at Mike's delinquent childhood and how he overcame so many seemingly insurmountable hurdles en route to winning the heavyweight championship under the guidance of Cus D'Amato, Bill Cayton, and Jimmy Jacobs, and I truly want to believe his bizarre conduct against Evander Holyfield was but a momentary lapse into insanity. I *want* to believe because of my intense love of boxing—my admiration for the countless good-hearted and good-natured fighters, trainers, cornermen, managers, and promoters from coast to coast.

We are family. And whenever someone cuts into the skin of boxing, we all bleed.

Of course, this guilt by association is prevalent in most professions. Because our society is one of extremes, for every Mother Teresa there's a Jeffrey Dahmer and for every Evander Holyfield there's a Mike Tyson. Finding that comfortable middle ground between the two is one of mankind's greatest challenges.

I have found mine, but it certainly wasn't easy. I am as comfortable standing between two brawling prizefighters as I am on the judicial bench. Yet I would not be in the enviable position of enjoying either had it not been for the education received from "the school of hard knocks" in my youth. The most valuable and enduring lessons I've ever learned were taught in a boxing ring.

Granted, boxing is not for everyone. Yet for me it opened doors that otherwise would have forever been closed. Because of the discipline of the amateur aspects of the sport that was instilled in me in the Marine Corps, boxing enabled me to attend college on an athletic scholarship. This was the initial step toward fulfillment of my dreams—law school, becoming a district attorney, and, eventually, a district court judge.

Indeed, boxing is the thread that runs through my life, and I am not overstating the issue when I say I love it. As a discipline, it taught me qualities I believe to be absolutely necessary to live a good, righteous life: courage, honesty, integrity, responsibility, persistence, and loyalty, to name just a few. Hopefully, as we journey through this unique world of hard hands and equally as hard heads, through the magnificent arena that is so close to my heart, that which I always refer to as "the discipline," you will be able to judge for yourself.

Only then, I believe, with the facts firmly in hand, will you be able to make an honest assessment as to whether our profession is the "sweet science" we contend it to be, or the "blood sport" of our detractors.

For now, though, I must address the universal shame. There is no justification whatsoever for Mike Tyson's behavior on that fateful night of June 28, 1997. His lack of civility embarrassed everyone, all of humanity.

Two's Company, Three's a Crowd

Oliver McCall was whimper-ing. His eyes were filled not only with tears but also with a hopelessness I'd never seen before in a prize-fight ring. His was the look of a man who had just heard terrible news.

I had to stop and pinch myself. Surely I was reading too much into it. This wasn't really happening. He was playing possum, trying to draw Lennox Lewis into a trap. He was suckering him into dropping his guard for the briefest of moments, and then he would turn Lewis's lights out with a heavy right to the head.

But the more I thought about it, the more it seemed that McCall wasn't acting. Nobody, not even Marlon Brando, could put on that convincing a performance. His tears were real, spilling from his eyes and rolling down his cheeks. His hands were motionless, dangling at his sides. He was defenseless, hopelessly alone in the loneliest sport of all.

It was February 7, 1997, just seconds before the start of the fifth round of the scheduled twelve-round championship bout for the vacant WBC heavyweight title, and Oliver McCall, the former champion, was blubbering like a baby.

Earlier in the fight he had left me speechless when he dropped his arms and simply walked away from Lewis. At the time, I figured he was just frustrated. He had rushed Lewis a couple of times and unloaded a few punches, which Lewis easily brushed aside. McCall could not match Lewis's strength, and he was losing the battle inside. He was unable to close the distance and connect. Lewis simply tied him up. He appeared to be hopelessly outmatched, and his frustration mounted as the fight progressed.

Before the start of the third round, McCall did not go to his corner. Instead, he paced back and forth, as if in a daze. Strange, yes. But I honestly thought his behavior was an act—a bizarre sort of psych-job.

But once the fourth round had concluded, I knew better. When McCall had staggered back to his corner, I approached him, got down on one knee, and, as gently and as gentlemanly as I could, I said, "Son, something is wrong with you. Can you tell me what it is?" His eyes were glistening with tears as he looked at me briefly, then down at the canvas. His lips were quivering and then he began to cry.

I looked over at George Benton for an answer. But the veteran trainer, who was leaning against the ropes to my right, was as baffled as I was. Benton shook his head sadly and looked away; he didn't know what to say either. And then Greg Page, Benton's assistant, started screaming at McCall: "Man, don't do this to yourself. Get in there and bust his ass. Don't do this shit to yourself. Get out there and fight."

I told Page to shut up, then turned back to McCall and said, "Are you okay, son?" He gave me a glazed stare. And then I asked, "Do you want to fight?"

McCall lowered his head, then slowly raised it and stared into the audience. He hesitated, as if swallowing his pride, and then said, "I gotta fight. I gotta fight."

It was as chilling a statement as I've ever heard. But my only option was to say, "Okay, son, let's try it again."

The fifth round began in brutal fashion. Lewis bashed McCall with a cross, then hit him with a right hand and moved in close. But McCall didn't even try to counter. His hands were down and he looked like a rag doll. I stepped in and broke them apart, and then Lewis nailed McCall again with a cross and another right hand. McCall's only defense was apathy. I immediately stepped between the fighters and stopped the fight.

I had no choice. Oliver McCall wouldn't or couldn't protect himself, so I had to do it for him.

I'm not being melodramatic when I say that McCall's bizarre behavior prior to the start of the fifth round still haunts me. When I asked him "Do you want to fight," he didn't respond right away. Instead, his eyes flitted into the darkness, into the void of indistinguishable faces sitting in the first five rows at ringside. I have no idea what or for whom he was searching, but the desperation and despair deeply etched in his face tore my heart out.

Some force, one so strong, so powerful that it dare not be denied, coerced Oliver McCall to enter the ring on February 7 against his wishes, against his better judgment. I can't prove this, but that's what I feel in my gut.

In my wildest dreams I know it could not have been George Benton or Greg Page who forced him to fight. Both are former fighters who are well aware of the fine line that separates physical well-being from serious injury. They would never subject a fellow fighter to unnecessary wrath. Their *only* concern is the health of their respective fighters. It could have been some high-roller sitting at ringside that night, such as Don King, McCall's promoter. I'm not going to bad-mouth him solely on suspicion and innuendo, but if I had the power, I would have given my left nut for the chance to question King as well as McCall's manager. And I would have preferred to do it in a court of law.

Of course, that's just wishful thinking on my part. There is no such tribunal in the business of boxing. With the exception of strong state boxing commissions such as those that exist in Nevada, California, New York, and New Jersey, the discipline lacks universal judicial exactness. There is no forum in which to render absolute justice. Sadly, redemption and retribution are not defined in the true legal sense, as most of us know it to be. In professional boxing they are simply physical means to a brutal end. And standing between this contradiction is the referee, one man trying his damnedest to sort out punches while attempting to sustain order within a disorderly framework.

The irony of the McCall-Lewis mismatch is that when I visited McCall's locker room prior to the fight to go over the rules, I saw someone full of braggadocio. George Benton, whom I consider one of the finest trainers in the business, was watching McCall tape his own hands. This was a bit strange, because the trainer or his second usually performs that task. But McCall was wrapping his hands and shouting, "Man, this fight ain't gonna go the distance. I'm gonna knock this guy out."

I told McCall to turn off the boom box. Once the circuslike atmosphere had subsided, I said, "Now, if the fight goes the distance . . ." McCall didn't even let me finish, shouting, "Man, this fight ain't goin' the distance. I'm gonna knock him out."

I said, "Okay, but if it goes the distance, will you touch gloves before the start of the twelfth round?"

McCall nodded and said, "Yeah, I'll do that. But you don't have to worry, ref. It ain't goin' no twelve rounds. I'm gonna knock him out."

We went back and forth like that as I went over the WBC rules. It was almost comical, because I had never seen anyone this confident. But I couldn't knock him for feeling like that. In the first Lewis-McCall fight, McCall rushed Lewis in the opening moments of the first round and popped him with a straight right hand, a sneak right hand at that, and—*bang!* Lewis crumpled. He managed to get back up, but his legs were wobbly and the ref stopped the fight. Lennox Lewis got knocked on his butt and, to everyone's amazement, Oliver McCall was the WBC world heavyweight champion.

And now, moments before the rematch, I figured McCall was merely basking in the excitement of the moment. I couldn't blame him. He'd earned the privilege.

Once the introductions were made and the fight began, it looked to me as if McCall was using the same strategy he'd used in the previous bout. He rushed Lewis and unloaded with the right

29

hand, but this time Lewis was ready for him. Lewis, the taller and stronger of the two, wasn't about to allow McCall to close the distance and slip in that punch. McCall tried two or three more times to land with his right, but he just wasn't up to the task.

That's when it appeared to me that McCall knew that, barring the unforeseen—an accident, if you will—he wasn't going to beat Lewis. And that's when his fragile world crumbled at his feet, leaving him with nothing but tears. I'm not a psychologist, but it sure as hell looked like a mental breakdown to me. All of which was even more bizarre than what Mike Tyson did to Evander Holyfield.

Although Mike regressed to dirty barroom tactics by biting Evander's ears, at least he was fighting—trying his damnedest to win, albeit with illegal moves. Oliver McCall psychologically collapsed. His mind shut down. An unknown force negated his physical powers and he simply refused to fight. It was so incomprehensible that I am unable to explain it.

No one, myself included, can really know what was going on in McCall's head, whether his breakdown was purely psychological or the residual effect of his drug abuse. McCall had been in rehab for this problem, and though he was clean for the fight, according to tests done after, we just don't know the long-term effect drugs can have on a person, even after a stint in rehab. Something was up with McCall, though, because prior to the fight the word on the street had been that he was in no shape to enter the ring.

It should be noted that "the word" is, at best, nothing more than a combination of suspicion and innuendo. Yet in professional boxing "the word" oftentimes is about as close to the truth as you are going to get.

What fact I do know was that Oliver McCall was in good physical shape, weighing in at 222 pounds. I distinctly remember his weight because of a brief conversation I had with Don King on the day before the fight. I was staying at the Vegas Hilton Hotel and had just gotten out of the elevator when King walked by and said hello.

When I cautioned him that it was not proper for us to speak, he said, "Yeah, I know. I respect that, Mills. But you know, my man weighs about 222 and Lewis weighs 252. I don't believe Lewis is in shape."

In retrospect, Lennox Lewis probably was a tad bloated—his best weight is 240. Nonetheless, he was, at the very least, mentally prepared for the challenge.

Sadly enough, Oliver McCall, Don King's *man,* was not.

∞∞∞∞∞

Inference is a damning tool. It is used quite a bit in the judicial system to link alleged lawless persons and lawless acts to one another. Too often vast areas of gray hinder the pursuit of due process. Seldom is wrong separated from right by clear-cut black-and-white facts. That's why I've often compared my work in the courtroom to what I do in a prizefight ring in this fashion: In the courtroom, it's a case of controversy, but it's legal reasoning. A fight is also a case of controversy, but it is the most basic of cases. It is black and white. That's one reason I love boxing. It's good for me to get away from all the posturing in court and get down to the basics.

Yet even the basics of boxing are sometimes difficult to grasp. For example, trying to keep an accurate accounting of the curious circumstances surrounding ownership of the WBC heavyweight crown is as taxing as anything the IRS could nail us with. To say the least, the title has changed hands in rather peculiar fashion in the past five years. Evander Holyfield lost the crown to Riddick Bowe in 1992. Bowe, in turn, renounced the title rather than defend it against top-ranked Lennox Lewis, who was awarded the honor without having thrown a punch. Lewis, in short order, lost the belt to Oliver McCall, who lost it to Frank Bruno, who lost it to Mike Tyson, who was stripped of the title for not defending it against Lewis, who reclaimed the vacant title in the rematch with McCall.

And that's just the WBC. Couple its mind-numbing inconsistencies with the equally as baffling inequalities of the other main sanctioning bodies—the WBA, WBO, and IBF—and boxing makes our federal bureaucracy appear efficient. Add to this the glut of lesser sanctioning bodies of what pundits call the "alphabet soup"— the WBU, WBB, WBF, IBC, IBO, IBA, NABO, NABF, USBA, NABU, and USBO—and you have a pugilistic maze, an endorsement process every bit as incomprehensible as the programming instructions on your standard VCR.

I will address the problems I have with the various sanctioning bodies later. For now, though, prizefighting's current state of disillusionment, which should not be confused with the sport's blatant deceit of the past, is best illustrated by the unconscionable spectacles of the Tyson-Holyfield and McCall-Lewis fights, plus the Henry Akinwande–Lewis title bout, which completes the troika of professional boxing's inane and insane.

When Oliver McCall broke down in tears I viewed it, more or less, as a sign of the times. After all, drug use is fashionable to some folks, despite the mental instability that accompanies it. And when Mike Tyson denigrated himself to the level of gnawing street thug, I saw it as a reflection of today's pampered professional athletes, the spoiled brats who believe that the rules don't apply to them because of their celebrity status.

Yet on July 12, precisely two weeks after Tyson's culinary habits got him into trouble, Don King sent Henry Akinwande through the ropes to face Lennox Lewis for the WBC title in Stateline, Nevada. Akinwande's exhibition left me speechless.

At 6-foot-7 with an 86-inch reach, Akinwande won the World Boxing Organization's version of the heavyweight title in 1996 with a third-round knockout of Jeremy Williams. In order for Akinwande to get a shot at Lennox's title, however, he had to abdicate the WBO crown. We were told that Akinwande, with a 32–0–1 record, was the top-ranked WBC contender. How he reached this pinnacle is somewhat suspect, because he was the No. 5 ranked WBC heavyweight in May, yet suddenly he became the mandatory title challenger without having fought during the interim.

Born in Dulwich, south London, Akinwande left Great Britain when he was eight and spent the next eleven years in Nigeria. Tiring of Africa, he returned to England and took up boxing under the tutelage of manager Mickey Duff. From Duff to Don King, which led, literally and figuratively, to the big dance with Lennox Lewis at Caesars Tahoe.

Akinwande entered the ring first. I remember looking over at him, then looking up at him, and seeing that unmistakable look in his eyes. There was no misinterpreting his terror. The last place he wanted to be was in that ring facing Lennox Lewis. But then Lewis entered the ring, generating the usual excitement, and I dismissed my misgiving.

You can draw whatever inference you want from what I saw mirrored in Akinwande's face. I know his intimidation wasn't from dope, because we took his urine after the fight. Medically, he was clean—as fit as a fiddle. On the surface, he was one helluvan imposing physical specimen—huge, well-muscled, and at the proper weight, with no extra flab on him. Of course, appearances can be quite deceiving. While Akinwande appeared to be as strong as a bull, once the bell rang he proved to be as meek as a lamb.

Lewis nailed him early in the first round with a couple of good licks and what little fight remained in the big stiff vanished. He would stick his left arm out at Lewis, then loop his right arm over Lewis's shoulder and snuggle up close. It was pathetic.

Akinwande persisted in clinging to Lewis, and when I stepped in to break the clinch, he would not let go. It got so bad that I called time and said, "Listen, son. When I say break and step back, you damned well better break and step back. Do you understand me? I want you to step back like this," and I'd show him how it was done, dropping my arms and taking the step back.

I looked up at him, exasperated as hell, and saw his head bob up and down. So I asked him again, "Now, do you understand what I'm saying?" Again, Akinwande nodded. So I figured he understood me. After all, we weren't talking about something very complicated.

The fight resumed, but Akinwande tied up Lewis again, waltzing around the ring, adhering to the champ like some sort of big leech. And when I grabbed hold of Akinwande's arm to pull him off, he danced me around the ring also. We must have looked like an Oreo cookie—Lennox to the left, Akinwande to the right, and me stuck in the middle. It got so frustrating that I wanted to pop Akinwande in the mouth. I withheld the urge, however, and tried my best to get him to make a fight of it. But it was a waste of time and energy.

Henry Akinwande had no fight in him. It was a sham and a damned shame, and I disqualified him in the fifth round.

What was even tougher to comprehend was that even when I chased him, he was clueless. "That's it, you're gone. It's over," I told him, pointing to his corner. He just stood there like a bump on a log, so I took hold of his arm and shoved him toward his corner. He had this stupid look on his face, the kind of expression that told me he didn't know what in the hell was going on, so I told him that I had disqualified him for refusing to fight. But even then, faced with the most damning evidence of all—the riotous booing of the Caesars Palace crowd—he had the gall to say, "I wasn't holding. I was trying to fight inside."

For the first time in my life, I didn't know what in the hell to say. I was so stunned that I couldn't even say "Bullshit."

His behavior was almost as embarrassing as Mike Tyson's fall from grace. On that night, Akinwande was no more the top-ranked heavyweight contender than I was.

I've seen plenty of stiffs during my years in the ring—journeymen who were nothing but dogs, guys who were looking for an easy way out. But I've never seen anything quite like this. Not with two guys who were, theoretically, ranked high in the discipline.

When someone on the street goes for the easy way, there's usually a vigilant police officer on hand to make a proper arrest. When the alleged felon is arraigned, he is charged with fraud. Where I come from, the sonofabitch gets a speedy trial, a guilty verdict, and a stiff prison sentence. Hard-working, law-abiding citizens should expect nothing less of our judicial system.

Of course, few doubted that inequity would not be served in Akinwande's case. Under a Nevada state law that went into effect the day before his big dance, Akinwande could have been forced to forfeit his entire $1 million purse, plus face the possibility of being suspended.

Money is an intangible. It comes and it goes. Mostly it disappears quicker than we would like it to. But what good is money when, while accumulating it, you fail to earn the respect of your peers?

Although the Nevada State Athletic Commission did not withhold Akinwande's purse, it did agree unanimously that I was correct in disqualifying him for not fighting. As such, the commission put a letter of reprimand in his file. By doing this publicly, what the commission *really* did was issue a warning to all promoters that Akinwande might pull this stunt again.

Because the prizefighting business is predicated on what you can produce, the real discipline of the Akinwande affair may very well be that no promoter will ever want to take a chance on him again, because they will be afraid that people won't pay to see him fight. That's the real hammer. As a practical matter, Akinwande suffered a universal lack of respect as a fighter.

In the nebulous world of prizefighting, comprehending the subtle truth is sometimes as difficult as finding a legitimate WBC heavyweight contender.

Indeed, it may be that there was a dark cloud hovering over my head in 1977, because the brunt of professional prizefighting's bizarre crap that year occurred when I was the referee. Who, for instance, can forget "Fan Man," the idiot paraglider who dropped into the ring during the seventh round of the Holyfield–Riddick Bowe II title fight on November 6, 1993, at Caesars Palace in Las Vegas. Talk about a raft of snakes and bats.

This was one helluva battle, one of the better bouts I have ever worked. Holyfield opened two cuts on Bowe's forehead in the early going, then staggered him in the fifth with a crushing combination followed by a right-left-right barrage. This pummeling continued through the sixth round. And then with 1:50 left in the seventh, that nitwit came floating in out of the dark and landed in the ring ropes.

The only redeeming thing about "Fan Man's" unexpected entrance was that the sonofabitch landed in Bowe's corner. At the time, Rock Newman, Bowe's manager, was not in a jovial mood. "Fan Man" ended up getting the shit kicked out of him by Newman and a handful of Bowe's people before the bout was resumed.

Yet this was but a mere blemish on boxing's facade. A knucklehead wearing a parachute is nothing compared to what Oliver McCall, Mike Tyson, and Henry Akinwande inflicted upon us— three foul bouts that cause even our staunchest supporters to squirm with revulsion.

∞∞∞∞∞∞

A man is nothing if he does not stand up for what he believes in. If you've devoted your heart and your soul to someone or something, if you've invested your time and your energy as well as your faith and every ounce of goodwill into a person or a profession, then I believe you have a right to be upset when idiots hurt that which you love most.

My heart ached for Oliver McCall. It hurt for different reasons when Mike Tyson and Henry Akinwande dragged prizefighting through the gutter. In both instances, I wanted to slap them upside the head and scream, "Dammit, start acting like a man." Instead, better judgment took control and I did what was expected of me, disqualifying them for blatant disregard of boxing protocol.

As weird as those fights were, though, the fact that so many people wanted to put me on a pedestal for doing the right thing is even weirder. Then again, viewing much of society as what it has become—selfish, apathetic, unfaithful, disrespectful, shameless, disloyal, and undisciplined—I suspect my actions were a bit unusual. I didn't back down. I didn't cower or compromise my principles. Of course, it's easy to do what I did when you've got right on your side.

But I'm still somewhat uncomfortable with the celebrity status that has been afforded me out of the misfortune of others. Oliver McCall had a mental breakdown, Evander Holyfield lost a chunk of his ear, and Henry Akinwande lost the respect of his peers by refusing to fight. And simply because I was there doing nothing more than the job I was expected to do, a lot of people started calling my actions heroic. That's the most bizarre twist of all.

It started moments after I disqualified Tyson, when security personnel whisked me out of the ring to safety. That's when the media descended upon me in droves, treating me as if I were royalty. It seemed as if every television and radio station in the world interviewed me. There was no letup whatsoever in the hours after the fight, little letup in the days that followed.

I'd be a fool to say I didn't enjoy it; it was a real kick in the butt. But what the media focused on stunned me. Everyone seemed enamored by the fact that I got in Tyson's face. Just because I told Tyson I didn't believe him, all of a sudden I'm some hotshot badass. It's all sort of ridiculous, really. My comment to Tyson was just a natural reaction. It's what I would say to anyone who's pissing in my ear while trying to convince me it's raining.

My approach to life has always been: "Balls to the wall—charge! What you see is what you get; nothing more, nothing less." Am I tough? Damn right I am. I'm the product of tough times—I'm *Semper Fi,* Mac, so back off. If you've got a problem with that, tough shit. I stand up for what I believe in. I say what I think. And if you're looking for some fence-sitting, hand-wringing, politically correct sorry excuse for a man, then you've approached the wrong guy.

With that in mind, maybe you can understand why I was stunned when, time and again, I was asked: "Weren't you afraid that Tyson would attack you? Surely once you saw what he did to Holyfield, you must have been afraid he'd go after you."

What was there to be afraid of? I was right; Tyson was wrong. End of discussion. But, of course, it didn't die that easy. It took a bit of explaining, but I believe I got my point across.

Physically speaking, I'm not a big man. I stand 5-foot-7 and weigh 146 pounds, the same weight I fought at 40 years ago in the Marine Corps. But even at my advanced age I can handle myself. If you get in my face, I will get right back in yours. Try to muscle me and I'll cut you off in no uncertain words.

So, when someone asks if I was afraid of Mike Tyson, my honest answer is that it never even entered my mind. I was in the prizefight ring that night to do a job, a job that I love. I wasn't thinking about being a celebrity. I did not enter that ring with the express purpose of waving hello to my mama back in Savannah, Georgia. I was there to uphold the rules and regulations as set down by the Nevada State Athletic Commission. And when Tyson ran afoul of good order, when he stepped outside the lines of protocol, I disqualified him. After the second bite, I did not have to give any thought to the matter at all. He violated the rules and I chased him, pure and simple. Fear was never a factor.

As a matter of fact, I'm a firm believer that when you stand up for what's right—when you are doing exactly what good conscience dictates—you have nothing to fear but fear itself.

Granted, there's not much originality to my way of thinking. My father taught me the value of hard work, and the Marine Corps expanded that education. It was in the Corps that I learned how to be a man, a man of principle. Discipline, self-respect, respect for others, persistence, pride, loyalty, courage, honor—these are the qualities the Marines drove home. In condensed form, it boils down to the simple fact that you've got to be true to yourself.

Another thing the Marines taught me is that men and women—*real* men and women—take responsibility for their actions. Not only do they know how precise is the line separating right from wrong, they also know the stern consequences for deviating from a given set of rules. Given a job to do, no matter how difficult it may be, reliable individuals attack it and successfully carry out their mission within a framework of strict law and order. In return, all they expect is a sincere "Job well done" from their superiors. They're not expecting medals or parades, full-blown stories written about them or television appearances.

More than anything else, though, a responsible person realizes that the adoration of "hero" is reserved for someone who, for example, sacrifices his or her life to save the life of a child. Heroes go above and beyond a given call of duty.

I am not a hero. I'm simply flesh and blood, a man who has tried at all times to do his best while attempting not to repeat the mistakes of yesterday. In that regard, I'm far from perfect. In fact, I screwed up badly in the Tyson fight and I thought everyone would nail me to the wall for it. When I allowed my mouth to override my brain seconds after that first bite and said I was going to disqualify Tyson, I put Marc Ratner in a bad light. Some people have even accused Marc of overruling me, but that wasn't the case. Once Dr. Homansky gave me his medical opinion, the call was mine to make. And I chose to allow the fight to continue.

Of course, that does not justify my error. I simply should not have said anything about disqualification until I was in possession of all the facts. I should have kept my mouth shut and instigated a proper investigation. What bothers me is that I know better. I simply screwed up.

Another point that needs to be clarified is that not once did Evander Holyfield question my decision to allow the fight to continue after that first bite. Always the consummate warrior, Evander's primary concern was the damage inflicted upon his ear. And once his handlers stopped the bleeding, he resumed the fight without protest.

But I am convinced that had this happened to anyone other than Evander Holyfield, I would have been faced with one very tough decision. If Don Turner, Holyfield's trainer, had said, "My man has lost a piece of his ear, and he's not going to fight," I would have had no choice but to say, "You'll fight or else . . ."

God help us if that scenario had presented itself. I believe that Marc Ratner would have gone to Holyfield's corner and said, "Look, the ref said go on. If you don't, you're going to lose the title."

But Holyfield, one of the greatest champions and classiest human beings I've ever been around, was not about to hide behind an excuse. Not even a badly damaged ear. It never entered his mind. He was there to defend his title and, by God, that's exactly what he did.

If you really want to know why I love the discipline as much as I do, you need look no farther than to Evander Holyfield.

ᗢᗢᗢᗢᗢᗢ

Jay Leno also is a class act. But I'd be lying if I told you that appearing on *The Tonight Show* didn't make me nervous as hell. I really didn't know what to expect. But it turned out to be a real great time, especially chatting with Leno. Talk about someone being a super nice guy, an up-front guy. His nose wasn't out of joint like you might expect with a hotshot television celebrity.

In fact, a bunch of us old fighters from the University of Nevada-Reno started a charitable project called the Jimmie Olivas Fund, named for the now-deceased former coach of our boxing team. One of the ways we're raising money is selling ballcaps embossed with "Let's Get It On." So, Mike Martino, who keeps track of the funds we raise, wanted me to present Jay with one of the hats. But when I arrived on the set, some of Leno's people hemmed and hawed, saying they didn't want me to do it. That's when Jay pulled me aside and said, "Listen, just do it. My people don't want you to do it because, before you know it, everybody will be coming onto the show and bringing me something. With you, though, it's okay. Just do it."

So when I made my entrance that night, I was wearing the hat. And when I took it off and handed it to Leno, he thanked me and placed it on his head. Talk about a perfect gentleman, a nice man, and a first-rate guy—he's class with a capital *C.*

It's funny, but I really didn't know what to expect from the *Tonight* people when I got off the plane about two hours before airtime. The whole thing was foreign to me. But then I saw this gentleman holding a sign with my name on it. And when I introduced myself to him, he said, "Oh, Mr. Lane, it's a privilege to have you in my car. This is really an honor." Hell, I told him the honor was all mine. I sat up front with him in the limousine and we had a great time talking boxing for a while. The guy was real knowledgeable, a fan. He was from Hungary, and he knew his fighters.

So now we're driving around and he said, "Mr. Lane, we've got some time to kill, so I'd like to give you a tour of Beverly Hills." Well, I'm not much into touring. And to be honest with you, I didn't really give a shit about Beverly Hills. But he drove me around pointing out all those $4 million homes of the famous movie stars. The best part of all, though, was spending time with the driver. He was just a nice man, and I thoroughly enjoyed his company.

As for *The Tonight Show* itself, the toughest part was making sure I didn't let something slip out of my mouth before my brain could clean it up—you know, like I did on *The Larry King Show.* It aired shortly after Tyson made a public spectacle of himself. I sort of did the same thing when Larry King asked about the conversation I had with Tyson after that first bite. I told him that Tyson said it was a punch, and that I disagreed with Tyson's interpretation of the facts.

KING: *Tyson said to you it was a punch?*
ME: *He told me it was a punch, and I said—you want me to say what I said? Maybe I'd better not say what I said.*
KING: *You can say whatever you like.*
ME: *I told him that was bullshit.*

I thought all the production people in the television studio back in Reno were going to have a heart attack, they were laughing so hard. But what the hell—I warned King that my exact words might not be fit for family consumption. But he challenged me. Once the camera was turned off, I toasted him with a coffee cup full of beer and a handful of nuts, which cracked up the guys in the studio even more.

What few people know is that once I got to the studio and everything was set up for the show, one of King's people asked me what I'd like to drink. I told him I wanted a beer and some nuts. He said, "Oh, I'm sorry, but you can't have a beer. You're going on the air with Larry King."

My response: "Well, I want some beer and some nuts."

Someone ended up making a beer run, so I kicked back and drank a few Budweisers and ate some nuts. I was having a helluva good time. But I guess someone must have called King, because that production guy came up to me and said, "Larry King says you can't drink beer on the set."

I told him, "The hell I can't."

Next thing I knew, someone handed me a coffee cup and I poured the beer into it. Nobody else said a damned thing, and the show went on.

Hey, Larry, this Bud's for you.

Discipline: The First Step Toward Success

Although I had the best motivational teachers in the world, you won't find any of their self-help books in the library. That's not meant to demean their brilliance, though. In fact, the life-sustaining lessons these gentlemen imparted to me were every bit as inspirational as anything you might receive from Norman Vincent Peale.

I speak of Sergeants J. Doyle, T. Groves, R. L. Adams, and J. R. Owen, the ramrods of Platoon 266, Fourth Battalion, Marine Corps Recruit Depot, Parris Island, South Carolina. You'll have to excuse the use of initials; we weren't on a first-name basis. In fact, we were never allowed to address them other than by the title "sir" or "drill instructor." Their mission wasn't to be my buddy or my friend. The DI's sole goal is to build Marines—disciplined, highly conditioned, and trustworthy members of a team—out of lackadaisical, soft, ill-mannered, disorderly, and selfish civilians. To say the least, it's a life-altering transformation.

Despite the lapse of forty-one years, if I were to meet one of my old drill instructors on the street today, I'd snap to attention and address him with the respect he deserves: "Sir, Private Lane, serial number 1611770, requests permission to speak, sir." And then I would be petrified that my shoes weren't shined well enough or that my shirt and trousers weren't squared away. The only thing I wouldn't have to fret about would be the regulation Marine Corps white-sidewall haircut. My head has been GI for decades.

My roots run deep into the sand of Parris Island. In my mind I'm still an eighteen-year-old, kick-ass Marine. I'm *Semper Fi* to the day I die. And because I am, I still cling tightly to the hard lessons taught me by my DIs, who broke me down and then rebuilt me in the image of what the Corps still refers to as a "Marine's Marine." Which is simply a person—male or female, black or brown, red or white—who prefers to journey on the road less traveled.

Instead of taking the easy way out, ducking responsibility, and shirking my duties or making excuses for any failures, the Marines instilled in me a handful of life-altering principles—honesty, integrity, humility, hard work, persistence, and loyalty—that have not only made a difference in *my* life, but also to the countless hundreds of thousands of other young men who, over the years, have earned the right to wear the uniform. It's been that way since 1775, when the first recruit sauntered through the door of Tun Tavern.

In a word, I'm speaking of discipline. And discipline is what boxing, and life, is all about.

While boxing definitely is not for everyone, it has been a large part of my life. It is the one thread that runs through my yesterdays to the present, connecting the young Marine Corps boxer I was in 1958 to the kindly old judge I am today.

I first learned the discipline from two of the best boxing scholars I have ever known: Sergeants Coston Donahue and Harold Williams. Because these two black coaches took me under their protective wings on Okinawa and drilled home the unique qualities it takes to be a disciplined fighter, I can honestly say that whatever success I enjoy today I owe, in large part, to the hard lessons they taught me.

The Corps taught me to respect myself, and Sergeants Donahue and Williams built upon that foundation. They taught me the value of conditioning, which is so necessary to being successful in the ring, and instilled in me the quality of not quitting on myself. "Nothing is impossible," Donahue once told me, "if you maintain your discipline, stay on your feet, and continue swinging."

I haven't forgotten those lessons nor has my love of boxing diminished, even though prizefighting is often tarnished by a handful of gutter trash. For the most part, the world of professional boxing is filled with some of the kindest, most endearing men and women I've ever known. And that, more than anything else, is why I firmly believe that prizefighting most definitely has a place in our society.

Recently, I was asked to clarify that statement as a guest of *ShowTime*. The segment began with me explaining the equipment involved and the correct way to punch—how you snap the jab, how turning the punch over at contact is very similar to a baseball player at bat when he snaps his wrists upon making contact with the ball. Then the interviewer pointed out that the television ratings of boxing matches had fallen, that it seemed as if fewer and fewer people were interested in the discipline, and he asked: "Why should anyone watch boxing?"

My response went something like this: If you don't like blood, don't watch it. But if you can get beyond your knee-jerk dislike and take a close look at the sport, you will see what legendary trainer Gil Clancy has called the most superior athlete in the world—the well-conditioned fighter. If you want to see courage under pressure and true determination, if you want to see someone transcend obstacles under difficult circumstances, then you owe it to yourself to watch a good competitive prizefight, because you will see the combination of all these magnificent qualities. In essence, what you will observe is an encapsulation of life's challenges.

Living is all about trying and succeeding under pressure, rising above that which you normally could not accomplish. And that simply means outworking the other sonofabitch.

If you are Ray Robinson, Ray Leonard, or Willie Pep, men blessed with all the moves and God-given athletic ability, then you've got the big edge—you are going to be the champion, no matter what. But if you do not have those gifts—if, for example, you have the limited physical tools of an Evander Holyfield, Rocky Marciano, Danny "Little Red" Lopez, or Joe Frazier—then you're faced with obstacles. Of course, you can overcome these barriers if you have the determination and a willingness to work hard. If you have that capacity, plus a fair chin and guts, then you can be every bit as successful as Robinson, Leonard, and Pep. At the same time, in order to give substance to your dream, you have to be willing to overcome fear, the biggest stumbling block of all.

But it can be accomplished. Anything can be accomplished if only you are willing to get in there and do it. And that, as I reiterated to those viewers of *ShowTime,* is what watching a good boxing match is all about. More to the point, it's what life is all about—overcoming your fears and self-doubts, getting your ears back, and *doing it* just like they taught us in the Marines.

There was never any discussion in the Corps about the merits of an order, no talking about the pros and cons. We were taught to do everything by the numbers. We exercised by the numbers, cleaned and maintained our weapons by the numbers, studied by the numbers, and even ate by the numbers.

We entered the mess hall in single file. Our chow was ladled onto our trays, and then we went to our appointed table and set down the tray. No one sat until the entire platoon was at the table. We'd stand at attention until the DI shouted, "Ready, sit." Usually, we didn't do this quick enough or in perfect unison, so the DI had us bouncing up and down until we got it right. We ate only when the DI shouted, "Ready, eat." There was no grab-ass, no conversation. We ate, and we *did it* in less than five minutes.

If we were on the obstacle course and encountered a wall, the DI would shout, "Climb over it," and we damned well *did it.* If we were at the rifle range aiming at the two-hundred-yard target, the DI would shout, "Shoot that sumbitch dead-center," and we *did it.* As such, doing it, whatever the task, simply became habit. And a damned good one at that.

Other than our DIs, the only thing we feared was failing to *do it* to the best of our ability.

When I was a fighter, I lived in fear of only two other things. I was afraid of stepping through the ring ropes and suddenly feeling the desperate urge of having to go to the bathroom. That's one helluva long walk back to the locker room under humiliating conditions. The other thing I feared was taking off my robe and not having my trunks on. I saw that happen once. The crowd was on its feet cheering, and then one of the boxers raised his arms in acknowledgment and took off his robe only to discover he was wearing nothing but his nut-cup. That's why I always checked four or five times to make sure my trunks were on before I left the locker room.

But I was not afraid of getting knocked on my butt, because the Marines taught me that there is no disgrace in that. Disgrace occurs only when you refuse to get back up. Nor was I afraid of getting hit, or the cuts and bruises that came from these punches. The Marines taught me that the surefire way of stopping my opponent from hitting me was to outsmart him—use a flanking maneuver, use speed and sound defensive measures, and then hit that sonofabitch harder than he hit you. If you don't believe that, then you definitely do not know your military history. You are unaware of what happened at Belleau Wood, Tarawa, and Iwo Jima; Inchon and the Chosin Reservoir; or Khe Sanh and Hue.

One of the toughest things in the world to defeat is a United States Marine with a well-defined mission. We'll keep coming at you and coming at you until victory is in hand. A Marine does not know *how* to quit. Of course, the same can be said for a Navy SEAL, Army Ranger, or Special Forces—elite fighting men one and all. But I neither swim nor have an affinity for berets, so I must confine myself to the few, the proud, the Marines.

I won't bore you with the usual rah-rah crap about boot camp. It was hell, and I have no desire to relive it. Out of the blood, sweat, and tears of that torturous ordeal was born the realization of who I was and what I was capable of doing with my life. First and foremost, I learned there were three ways of doing a task—the wrong way, the right way, and the Marine Corps way.

Punctuality was not arriving five minutes before a scheduled appointment. It was getting there a half-hour early. Physical fitness was not being able to run two miles in the noonday sun. It was running three miles with a forty-pound pack strapped to your back. Neatness was not merely putting on a clean uniform. It was making sure your haircut was regulation all the way, that you had showered and shaved and brushed your teeth, that your shoes were shined in such a fashion that they gleamed, and that the creases in your uniform were crisp. Responsibility was not merely saying "Sir, I do not know." It was saying "Sir, I do not know, but I will find out."

Above all, courage was not simply stepping forward when ordered, but being willing even when not commanded to do so.

I was taught to respect my fellow men and women, regardless of their religion or race. I was infused with a discerning loyalty to my country, regardless of political beliefs. I came to be faithful to my Corps, my comrades, and to myself. I discovered that you have nothing if you do not have honor.

These are lessons that run deep, lessons that become part of a Marine's identity. Let it suffice to say that there are countless hundreds of thousands of ex-GIs, but you'll seldom meet an ex-Marine. We are "former Marines." Although we exchanged our military lifestyle for that of the civilian world, the life lessons drilled into us by the Corps remain until our dying day. There is nothing "ex" about a Marine. Pride in our abilities, our accomplishments, and our beloved Corps is not something we easily forget. Honor, loyalty, brotherhood, courage, and persistence remain the cornerstones of our lives.

Once upon a time we learned to be true to ourselves and to others. That's the core meaning of *Semper Fi*. We discovered it was easier to stand firm and face the consequences than to cower or run away. We learned that bravery begins with honesty, that faith is fashioned from inner strength. We came to realize that liberty is priceless. As such, it must be defended no matter the cost—even if it means self-sacrifice.

The most valuable lesson instilled in me by the Marine Corps, though, was that you accomplish little without the help of others. Anyone who thinks he or she can get to the top without the aid of other people is a damned fool. Teamwork is the root of all successful ventures, whether it is in the family unit or in the workplace.

While military service might not be for everyone, the unbending lessons of regimentation are invaluable. It begins with discipline, which is absolutely necessary if you hope to surmount seemingly impossible conditions. The enemy of discipline is fear, and fear unchecked leads to panic. Any group that panics is no longer a disciplined unit; it is a mob. And mobs feed on themselves and are destroyed from within. A team, a well-disciplined unit, can face fear and overcome it by the sheer will and determination of numbers. The team can do this because of its intense obligation to self and comrades.

This country is the greatest example of that principle that I can think of. We are a varying race of people with varying religions and cultures, scattered throughout a vast homeland of fifty states of varying climates and geological formation. Yet we surmount difficulty hand in hand, brother to brother, sister to sister, sister to brother. As part of the whole, we are a vast, far-reaching family. On our own, though, we are isolated individuals desperately in need of help—assistance we know is ours for the asking, because brotherhood is an integral part of being an American. The United States has survived while lesser nations have been torn asunder because Americans are not selfish bastards.

So endeth the lesson. And now, if you would all please stand to attention and sing along with me: "From the Halls of Montezuma, to the shores of Tripoli . . ." Just kidding.

∞∞∞∞∞

Considering my family background and fortune, it might seem unusual that I would take the road less traveled—the Marines and boxing—en route to my present destination. I am, after all, the grandson of the man who created Georgia's Citizens & Southern Bank, the largest bank in the state. As such, *Semper Fi* was not meant to be part of my lexicon.

In late summer 1956, my future had been precisely planned. My father, Remer, had already made up his mind that I was going to attend the University of Michigan. We flew to Detroit, rented a car, and drove to Ann Arbor, and then we sat down with the dean of the College of Agriculture. Despite my average grades at Middlesex—the Concord, Massachusetts, preparatory school I attended from age twelve to eighteen, I was accepted at Michigan. My future was carved in stone.

My daddy had also taken the necessary steps to make sure I would be comfortable at Michigan. Tuition, room and board, books, and a monthly allowance would be part of the deal. I would major in agriculture and forestry, and then return home to Combahee, my father's eleven-thousand-acre South Carolina plantation.

Or, if I tired of farming, I would pursue the family banking business.

My grandfather, Mills Bee Lane, for whom I am named, started the C&S Bank in 1887 and made it the biggest and most prosperous bank south of the Mason-Dixon Line. My father, on the other hand, chose a different path to ensure his affluence. Like his father before him, my daddy was a man of vision, a strong-willed individual who was not afraid to roll up his sleeves and get his hands dirty pursuing his dreams. But my daddy wanted no part of banking. His heart wasn't in it. He wanted to be a farmer, and his concept of enjoyment was making the soil work for him. As such, he purchased Combahee from the DuPont family and subsequently raised cattle, baled hay, and worked the long rows of timber on his plantation.

My hang-up with farming is pretty well cut and dried. I worked the fields side by side with the hired hands. I baled hay, cut timber, and herded cattle from dawn to dusk. And then, during summer vacations from Middlesex, I repeated these tasks until I was eighteen. In essence, my daddy farmed all the farming out of me.

Banking, on the other hand, would not have been all that bad. And I've always had a good head for numbers—not that that would have really mattered. I was the grandson of the South's most proficient and prestigious banker, and I would not have had to worry

54

about gainful employment. But therein lies the problem, in my mind at least. No matter how well I did in that endeavor, I would never really know if I had reached the top because of my own abilities or because of my family name.

Which is how I ended up in Marine green instead of bib overalls or a three-piece suit. If nothing else, I am hardheaded, and I wanted to make my own decisions. It was my life and I was going to lead it as I saw fit. I wanted to be a boxer, a fighter. What better place to start than by joining the best damned fighting force on the face of the earth?

"Son, I think you should reconsider your options," my daddy said time and again. He was polite enough in his refusal, but I was not only sick and tired of farming but of school as well. So I kept arguing with him, day and night, about joining the Corps.

Finally, one miserably hot afternoon, I was working in one of our hay fields called Quarantine when daddy spotted our mailman, Mr. Stroup, who was in the National Guard, driving down the dirt road next to the field. My father pulled him aside and related to him my reluctance to attend college and my desire to join the Marines.

"Well, Mr. Lane," Stroup said, "every now and then when a young man doesn't know what he wants to do, the military ain't so bad."

My daddy nodded, then turned to me and said, "Mills, you still want to go into the Marine Corps?"

When I told him I did, he said, "All right, you get your butt home and change your clothes, and you go to Savannah and enlist right now before I change my mind."

I said, "Yes sir. I'm gone." That was on August 13, 1956. Three days later I was at Parris Island getting my head shaved and being issued my Marine gear while four of the biggest, meanest drill instructors in the Corps screamed: "Faster, faster. Hurry up, hurry up." I was scared to death and wondering why in the hell I hadn't listened to my daddy.

For thirteen weeks we never walked anywhere—we ran all the time. It was thirteen weeks of getting screamed at, slapped around, and cursed at. Thirteen weeks of running, jumping, climbing, and endless physical training, which they called PT. We marched as a team and we drilled as a team. And when one individual screwed up, every member of the platoon paid the price for that transgression by being corrected and punished as a team. You name it and we did it in unison.

There were no individuals—only the platoon. Seventy-two scared shitless boots being molded into one cohesive unit. And when it was over, having survived, we were proud to claim the title of United States Marine.

Boot camp was a kick in the ass, both figuratively and literally.

∞∞∞∞∞

Saying that the Marines build men and women is as much an understatement as it is superficial. What the Corps really does is acquaint the individual with the physical and mental abilities we are all born with. That this introduction is not done in a "warm and fuzzy" manner is what sets a Marine above your everyday soldier or sailor.

The Corps teaches you to stand on your own two feet. Because of the training every boot receives, you discover that in times of stress or peril you can reach deep down inside yourself and grab hold of the innate qualities all men and women possess—an undeniable will to win, no matter how hopeless the situation appears; the will to survive, no matter how desperate the circumstance. You become a "doer," an overcomer.

Through the combined efforts of my DIs, the Corps turned me into a combat fighting machine. My boxing coaches, Sergeants Donahue and Williams, built upon this, taking my physical skills, heart, and desire and channeling them into the confined area of the boxing ring. While their teaching was as intense as it was thorough, once I climbed through the ring ropes the battle was mine alone.

"We can only do so much," Williams told me over and over. "We can teach you the basics of defense and how to effectively throw your punches. But once you get eyeball-to-eyeball with that other sonofabitch, it's just you and God almighty. Either you kick his ass or he kicks yours. When the bell rings, there's nothing more I can do to help you."

And that, in a nutshell, is what boxing is all about. All the hours of training—the running, sparring, and work on the heavy and light bags—all boils down to perilous three-minute conflicts between two individuals who have been afforded an equal opportunity of turning themselves into the best boxers they can be. That I was raised in a wealthy environment as a child didn't mean a thing. The guy trying to outpoint or knock me out didn't give a shit if my granddaddy was a banker or that my daddy owned a plantation.

My mama and daddy weren't in that ring with me. Neither were those highbrow teachers at Middlesex. Sergeants Donahue and Williams weren't there either. It was just me and me alone. I would succeed or fail on my own merits. And that's why I'm so proud of winning the Marine Corps All-Far East welterweight championship in 1958 while stationed at Camp Sukiran on the island of Okinawa in the East China Sea. I proved to myself that I could accomplish the most difficult of tasks on my own merits.

Being stationed with the 3rd Marines on Okinawa meant one thing: endless combat training. But I was fortunate to serve under a regimental colonel who loved boxing. When the word went out that our battalion boxing team needed volunteers, I jumped at the opportunity. It was the culmination of a childhood dream. During my senior year at Middlesex, I had wanted to compete in the Golden Gloves tournament in Boston, but the school's headmaster thought such an endeavor would be demeaning. So the closest I came to fulfilling my dream was sparring sessions with the other students.

But living the life of a boxer was far more strenuous than I had imagined. Being a Marine means always being in top physical shape. But being in shape for combat is not the same as being in shape to box. Running three miles a day with a field pack is one thing. Running five miles in addition to that is sheer torture. But I was quick to learn the physical price one must pay to become a top-notch boxer. I did the extra roadwork to increase my lung capacity and to strengthen my legs. I did hundreds of sit-ups each day to harden my stomach. I worked endlessly on the heavy and light bags to develop upper-arm strength, quickness, and dexterity. I jumped rope until I was dizzy with fatigue. I sparred with veteran fighters, getting whacked over and over again until I learned how to slip their punches and counter with my own. And when these lessons were learned, I climbed through the ring ropes and fought my way to the All-Far East welterweight title. I did it, by God—I *did it.*

But no matter what your profession, there are always some bastards who take delight in making your life miserable. In my company that man was a sergeant we called "Big Bella," and he was as big a prick as I ever encountered in the Corps. Because I was but a mere PFC, it seemed as if the sergeant was jumping on my butt day and night. I don't know what his problem was, but whenever I started to leave the company area to begin training for the boxing team, he was there to read me the riot act. I think the guy had a problem with living, so he was going to do his damnedest to make sure everyone else had it tough, too.

To my rescue came Ron Beagle. He was my lieutenant. More to the point, he was everything Marine Corps leadership is meant to be. Lieutenant Beagle played end for the Naval Academy football team. He was as tough as nails, but fair. The bottom line is he was the kind of leader you would follow into hell and back—the sort of person you'd risk your life for.

When Beagle heard that the sergeant was harassing me, he pulled the jerk aside and said, "You get off Lane's ass and leave him alone. This is your first and last warning." Beagle did not have to say anything else. Next thing I knew, all I had to worry about was the other boxer trying to knock my head off. "Big Bella" had been neutered and life became somewhat easier. But only because someone else thought it important enough to help me out.

That's why I can't stress strongly enough the fact that no matter how successful you may become, you didn't get there without the help of others. When you think about it long enough, you come to realize that every "Big Bella" in our lives is countered by a Lieutenant Beagle. While the lieutenant's intervention had nothing to do with what I eventually accomplished in the ring, he did a great job of clearing an obstacle standing in the way of my eventual championship. Because common courtesy demands that I give credit where credit is due—and because my mama certainly didn't raise a dummy—I must thank Lieutenant Beagle, who made my life a whole lot easier. My gratitude also extends to my boxing coaches, Sergeants Donahue and Williams.

And while I'm at it, I've also got to give credit to Roscoe Arari, an older Okinawan gentleman who was always hanging around the gym and giving me pointers during training. I really appreciated his help, although almost no one else did. In their eyes, Roscoe's failing was that he wasn't an American.

One of the truly sad things about any army of occupation is the feeling of superiority over the local population that becomes ingrained into the warriors. This haughtiness certainly is not taught. I believe it is simply one of the ugly residues of war. In the instance of Okinawa's citizens, because they just happened to be born and raised on what became a vital part of the Japanese empire, the tendency of many Americans stationed there was to treat them at times like war criminals.

Roscoe and I talked at length, sharing our love of boxing, our dreams and ambitions, our likes and dislikes. I saw him as a friend, a kindly gentleman—not as a "Nip" or a "stinkin' Jap," as some of my fellow Marines called him. Roscoe was neither the enemy nor the object of my ridicule. Instead, he was an honest, sincere, hardworking man unafraid to extend his friendship and wisdom to a foreigner.

For the most part, though, our conversations were small talk. Nothing weighty. We sure as hell weren't philosophers; at least I

wasn't. So the bulk of what we bounced off each other was no different from what you'd share with any good friend, Asian or
American. Roscoe worked odd jobs and was saving his money.
Someday he hoped to buy some land and become a rice farmer. In
turn, I told him about my childhood days working the fields of my
daddy's farm and how that would be the last thing I'd ever do again.
Roscoe merely smiled and nodded his understanding.

We never talked about Okinawa's political climate or the
social barriers that stood between us. I believe that was more out
of Roscoe's respect for our friendship than anything I did. After
all, my focus was boxing, not international relationships. Yet with
the wisdom of age I can't help but wonder now what he had
endured. Roscoe was nineteen when the U.S. Army and Marines
assaulted his homeland in April 1945, no older than I was at
the time we became friends. Okinawa was the last great battle
of World War II—eighty-three days of hell in which 110,000
Japanese and 12,000 Americans died. Surely Roscoe must have
been involved in that horrible ordeal in some capacity. But we
never spoke of it. It was as if it had never happened. All that mattered was our friendship.

To a lot of Marines I served with, though, Okinawa's people
were no better than the Japanese. I always thought that odd, because
not only had the war been over for twelve years, but those who
indulged in racial hatred hadn't even fought there. In my estimation,
those Marines were screwed up. It doesn't take much intelligence to
hate. Only a damned fool gets caught up in that. Besides, the old
hands—those Marines who had actually fought the Japanese,
whether on Guadalcanal or Okinawa—were always the first to
praise the fighting ability of their enemy. To a man, these veterans

said that the Japanese soldier was every bit as tenacious as his American counterpart. The Japanese died fighting for what they believed in, and they did so just as heroically as did our young men.

I enjoyed Roscoe Arari's company. He was a friend in a very foreign land, and I still consider it an honor to have known him. He was a bright light in an oftentimes dark period in my life, because simply being a Marine was tough enough. But being a boxer on top of it was pushing endurance to the max.

While Sergeants Donahue and Williams worked my butt off in the gym, Roscoe stood off in a corner and watched my suffering with a knowing smile. And when the workout was completed, he would buy me ice cream and share his wisdom. The man loved boxing and had been a fair amateur in his youth. Whatever lessons he'd learned in life, the most important was being aggressive. Passivity, he said, gained you little. Because of our similar combative styles, Roscoe constantly encouraged me by saying, "No matter what anyone else tells you, you must always keep on your opponent. Don't ever back up. Keep going forward. Remain on the attack and your opponent can do little to hurt you." And then he'd take me aside, assume the boxing stance and show me how it was done—moving forward, sliding his feet in such a fashion as to always maintain balance and a proper defense.

I learned a lot from Roscoe Arari. His style became my style. In essence, despite the difference in nationalities, as fighters we became one and the same. And because we did, I kicked ass all the way to the All-Far East welterweight title.

En route to adding substance to my dreams, however, I learned one more valuable lesson. And a frail-looking, bug-eyed Air Force dude named Bill Wilkinson imparted it to me.

In late 1957, I was fighting as a light middleweight, even though Sergeant Donahue felt I was a perfect welterweight. Donahue wanted me to shed the extra weight and maintain myself at 146 pounds. He felt confident I could become a champion at that weight, but I had my doubts. I thought I was invincible the way I was.

I don't know this to be fact, but I suspect Sergeant Donahue felt I needed some convincing. We were working out at a gym in Shuri, and Donahue approached me and pointed to Wilkinson, who was standing at ringside, and said the kid wanted to fight me.

I took one look at Wilkinson and it was all I could do not to laugh. He was wearing glasses so thick they looked as if they had been fashioned from the bottoms of two Coke bottles. His eyes were so magnified that they resembled the eyes of a big fish. Wilkinson was white—a pale, sickly white. And he was tall and rangy, without a big muscle on him. What you have to understand is that I had been fighting some real tough guys. And now, all of a sudden, Sergeant Donahue wanted me to go toe-to-toe with this weak-looking pushover of an Air Force guy.

"Shit," I told Donahue. "Let's get it on."

So we laced up the gloves and got ready to square off. But before we started to pound on each other, I strutted over to Donahue and said, "Stand by, Sarge, while I eat this fucking guy alive."

Donahue smiled knowingly and said, "Mills, don't ever under-estimate the enemy."

Bullshit, I thought as I started stalking Wilkinson. Confident as ever, I moved in close and—*whack!* He nailed me underneath with a solid shot to the ribs. Lucky shot, I told myself, so I moved in again and—*whack!* Wilkinson hit me with a left hook to the head. He continued to hit me in that fashion until I finally wore him down in the third round and knocked him out. But until I managed to connect with that punch, that so-called frail-looking pushover made my life miserable.

All it took was a few stiff shots to my head and body, and my overconfidence was gone. And within a few weeks so were the extra pounds. I finally listened to Sergeant Donahue and became a welterweight—and the champion he knew I could be.

To this very day, whenever I see a fighter with big, thick muscles, I feel assured that the guy doesn't have much of a punch. But if he has long, smooth muscles like that bug-eyed fighter on Okinawa, then I know that fighter can really whack.

The most enduring lessons are often learned the hard way. Bill Wilkinson taught me to never *ever* judge a book by its cover.

∞∞∞∞∞∞

No matter where I go, people step forward and praise me for being different. They'll talk about their perception of my honesty, courage, or my ability to focus on a problem and eventually surmount it without giving up. While such praise is flattering, somewhere in the course of the conversation I become baffled because everyone wants an easy remedy to their own problems. They want to know what self-help books I've read over the years that helped me get to where I am today. It's as if they truly believe they can turn their life around by simply plunking down a few dollars for a book. If only it were that simple.

Because I'm nothing more than a simple ol' country boy, my answer is always the same: "I am what I am, pure and simple. What you see is what you get." Of course, because this response sounds a bit flippant and does nothing to clear up matters, I invariably end up talking about the Marine Corps.

To simplify matters, the Corps forced me to make discipline a habit—a *daily* habit, not something I use once a week or only when faced with difficulty. At the same time, boxing taught me how to succeed using these principles of discipline. And as I'll talk about later, these boxing lessons served me well throughout my professional life.

But you don't have to rush out and join the Marine Corps to be successful. And you sure as hell don't need to pull on a pair of boxing gloves to learn how to maneuver through and survive life's endless storms. What you do need to know, however, is a thing or two about discipline and how it can shape your life.

All journeys begin with a first step, and so it is with attaining whatever degree of success you desire. It begins with you. Until *you* begin to work on correcting *your* flaws, you will continue to face the same problems day in and day out. The root of all failure is the lack of individual discipline. You must identify what you like about successful people and apply those traits to your life. To do so, though, takes daily training, drill, and practice. It takes obedience and restraint. I can't do it for you. Neither can your mama or daddy. It's up to you and you alone. All I can do is pass on the wisdom that was drilled into me years ago at Parris Island. As my drill instructors were so fond of saying: *"Do it."*

I am not overstating the case when I say there is little difference between the discipline of prizefighting and the discipline you adhere to in your respective field of work. I don't care if you are a ranch hand in Montana, a shrimp fisherman in Louisiana, or work on the assembly line north, south, east, or west. If you lack personal discipline, you are going to get knocked on your butt. And without discipline, you sure as hell are less likely to get back on your feet.

I don't give a damn about how much education you have; B.A., B.S., or Ph.D. are just initials—they have about as much impact on your capacity to perform at the best of your ability as do the initials WBC, WBA, IBF, or WBO. More to the point, the world is overflowing with educated derelicts. I come across such fools every week in the courtroom.

No matter how good your skills are, you will not be a lasting success without self-control. Unless you're a psychopath, you clearly know the difference between right and wrong; you know what you should and should not do. Wavering or abandoning all that you know is right is setting yourself up for disaster. Although you might approach the top of your profession, you are in for the hard fall unless you possess obedience and restraint.

A disciplined fighter goes to his office—the gym—every day. Without fail, he does his roadwork and calisthenics, then pounds the heavy and light bags, spars a few rounds, then jumps rope and calls it a day. At home, he nourishes his body intelligently by watching what he eats. If he's a welterweight, he faithfully maintains his weight at 146 pounds. If he's a heavyweight and he does his best fighting at 226, he maintains that weight. What he doesn't do is balloon up to 260.

In essence, a disciplined fighter adheres to this regimen every week, day in and day out. He does not abuse his tools.

An excellent example of such a fighter is Ray Leonard. He walked away from the business for two years before making the big comeback against Marvin Hagler. Yet when Leonard returned he did not weigh more than 168. You can bet he had done a little running and had been to the gym and worked on the heavy bag, even though he did not *have* to.

Ray Leonard retired, yet he continued to tend to business. And that, in itself, is why he will go into the annals of prizefighting as one of the greatest of all champions.

The major failing of boxing is that almost 90 percent of the fighters do not attend to business, which totally baffles me. Although I will be going into that in greater detail down the line, the vast majority of today's prizefighters fail for the same reasons your coworkers or your bosses fail—they abuse their tools.

I'm sure you know people in your line of work who do not keep up with the latest business trends. Not only do they not read a lot, but they are also cutting corners every time they turn around. For example, as a district court judge, I could simply sit on my butt and be every bit as lazy as anyone else. Who cares if the lawyers have spent a lot of time working on a summary judgment brief, using up a lot of their client's money? So I say the hell with it, I'm not going to bother to read that brief. I'm just going to go out and wing it.

What prevents me from doing this—from cheating the lawyer, his or her client, and myself—is my personal discipline. You *must* be true to yourself and to others, too. Common courtesy dictates as much. To do otherwise is not only abusing your tools, it's also a crime against your fellow men and women—taking advantage of someone who desperately depends on you.

It is a sad fact of life, though, that far too many people refuse to attend to business. And it is mirrored in all walks of life. I see it in fighters, in lawyers, in grocery store clerks, in husbands and wives and children. I'm talking about those who are impolite, slothful, and uncaring. It's the wife who ignores a flapping shutter or a leaky faucet, assuming her husband will pull out the tools when he gets home and fix it. It's the lawyer who sneaks out for a drink when he should be working his butt off on his client's case. It's the guy or gal at work who thinks nothing of making a personal long-distance telephone call on the company nut. It's the company president who lies to his employees, the military contractor who overcharges his government, the federal employee who pisses away the taxpayer's money.

It's everyone, everywhere, and it is such a damn shame.

Instead of taking the time to do the job right, far too many people cut corners and take the easy way out. The result is a half-assed job, which amounts to an inferior product, dissatisfied customers, and wasted man-hours.

But, of course, it's not you. You are not late for work, you do not call in sick simply because you don't feel like working, you do not put in thirty-six hours each week knowing you will still be paid for forty. You don't bitch and complain about management, you don't verbally stab your coworker in the back just because you want that promotion.

Instead, you show up for work with a smile on your face and attack your job as if your life depended on it. You do this because you believe that no job is undignified if performed with dignity. You know that no matter what you do for a living, people will respect you if you perform your given task in a gracious manner.

To me, the difference between success and failure is obvious. You get your ears back and *do it*. You get up off your butt and *do it*. If you're going to school and have a term paper due, you go to the library and complete the research, then you return home and *do it*. You don't need to have been in the Marine Corps to understand this way of living. Doctors, lawyers, carpenters, painters, writers— whatever your profession, you owe it to yourself to *do it*, whatever *it* is, to the best of your God-given ability.

I'm sixty, yet I still refuse to abuse my tools. Four days a week at five o'clock, the alarm rings. Dammit, that bed feels great. And besides, maybe I'm getting too old for this shit. So my choices are I say fuck it, roll over, and go back to sleep, or I get my lazy ass out of that bed and do those two miles out there on the road. It is my choice, but I make the right one—I roll out of bed and *do it*. And when I'm out there running, the first thing that comes to mind is: "Man, I beat it. I beat the inclination to be lazy."

I *did it*. Once again. Sure, it's a little thing. But the accumulation of life's little things is the difference between winning and losing.

I still shine my shoes every ten days. I still do my roadwork. I still hit the heavy and light bags. I *do it* because I am a firm believer in what the late Vince Lombardi once said: "Every time you lose, you die. And when you win, you're reborn." That may be stretching it a bit, but I do believe that every time you make yourself do whatever it is that has got to get done, you win—you prevail. And every time you convince yourself to let it slide, that you'll do it tomorrow, you fail.

To hell with failure. I don't want some esoteric jackass working with me. I want that guy or gal on my team who is willing to run that extra mile, throw that extra punch. The bottom line is I don't care if they have great tools. I want to know if they've got heart and soul and discipline. And if they do, then I know I can count on them, in the ring or out.

The School of Hard Knocks

There's no arguing the fact that of all the heavyweights I've ever seen, Muhammad Ali will always be the greatest. I speak not just of his boxing skills, but also of his generosity, his kindness and humanity, and his capacity to captivate the world long after his magnificent skills have deteriorated.

I have two lasting pictures in my mind of Ali. The first is that of the sleek, polished boxer of his youth as he rejoices in triumph over a prone Sonny Liston. This is how I wish to remember Ali. But the cruel specter of reality won't allow it, because the second image is that of the intensely ill old warrior, one arm immobilized by sickness, the other shaking as he struggles to lift the fiery torch that would ignite the Olympic cauldron at the 1996 Atlanta Games. This erosion of past greatness still blurs my eyes with tears.

I first met Ali in April of 1960 at the Olympic Trials held in the Cow Palace in San Francisco. He was known as Cassius Clay at the time, the AAU light heavyweight champion. He fought the U.S. Army's Allen Hudson, who had won the inner-service heavyweight championship three years running. Hudson had won the championship at 190 pounds, but had since dropped his weight to 178 so he could fight Clay at light heavyweight. There were a lot of boxing insiders who thought that Hudson could beat Clay, and he came damned close because, when they squared off against each other on the second night of the competition, Hudson knocked Clay down in the second round. Of course, Clay didn't stay down long and eventually defeated Hudson on a technical knockout in the third and final round.

I know this sounds silly, but I still have the Olympic Trials program with all of the contestants' photos in it. One of my lifelong regrets is that I didn't have Muhammad Ali autograph his picture as Cassius Clay.

While Ali's past and present are the means to an end, there are those who feel as if he has somehow been tragically cheated. They feel that if Ali had not had to deal with the accumulation of a lifetime of punches to the head, he would be able to live a normal life today. While there is no arguing the physical reality of that line of thinking, clinging to such a premise is to summarize the universe after having viewed only a single snapshot. It's as simplistic and naïve as saying John F. Kennedy would still be alive today had he stayed in the Navy instead of going into politics.

Had Muhammad Ali not become the three-time world heavy-weight champion, possibly the greatest heavyweight of all time, no one would give a damn whether he suffered from Parkinson's disease and the likelihood of pugilistic dementia, the medical term for having taken too many blows to the head. Had Ali chosen a less punishing profession, he would have forever remained Cassius Clay—just another handsome, semiliterate black man mindlessly punching the clock at a menial job in Louisville, Kentucky.

Muhammad Ali will be the first to tell you that he would not trade his pugilistic past for a healthier present. "I have no regrets; none whatsoever," the world's most recognized man once told me. As well he shouldn't. With the possible exception of President Kennedy, no one in the past four decades has been held in such high regard.

Ali was a fighter, pure and simple. Unlike so many of today's professional athletes, he wasn't interested in cashing in on his fame through television commercials. He didn't merchandise his image, because his soul wasn't for sale. Muhammad Ali wasn't about money. Whether or not you agree with his political stance on the Vietnam War, and personally I do not, Ali was a man who functioned solely on the courage of his convictions, fighting anyone and everyone. And he did a damned good job of it, even when squaring off in a one-sided fight against the combined might of the federal government.

On April 28, 1967, at the height of the Vietnam War, Ali refused induction into the Army on the grounds that he was a Moslem minister. At the time, he said he was fighting for the respect of his religion, not fighting his country. Of course, almost everyone else thought different. Within hours of Ali's refusal to participate in what he called "an immoral war," the WBA and WBC stripped him of his crowns and state boxing commissions nationwide rescinded his boxing licenses. Less than two months later, he was convicted by a federal jury in Houston, Texas, of violating the Selective Service Act and sentenced to five years in prison.

If you give Ali the benefit of the doubt regarding his political convictions, absolving him for refusing to serve his country, then you can justify calling him a true American hero. But I can't do that, because I believe in this country and everything it stands for. As such, while I can separate Ali's political beliefs from his accomplishments as a fighter, I still view the man as the sum of his actions in and out of the ring. My bottom line is that when your country calls, dammit, you answer the call of duty and step forward.

Of course, Ali did what he thought was right. He did not violate his principles by doing what would have been politically correct, even though the Army guaranteed that it would not send him to Vietnam. To his way of thinking, he did exactly what all Americans are encouraged to do: stand by your convictions and take the moral high ground. The choice he made, however, resulted in his being deprived of three of the most productive years of his life.

For the record, Ali's draft board classified him in 1964 as 1V, unfit to serve in the armed forces, apparently for failing the mental examination. Two years later, when the Army lowered its intellectual standards, Ali was reclassified 1A without being retested. His troubles didn't end until 1970 when the Supreme Court voted 8 to 0 to reverse his conviction, saying the government had erred.

Although nothing is gained by taking sides on the Vietnam War, I can't help but recall Rudyard Kipling's wisdom when writing many years ago about a subject that took the French and United

States twenty years to figure out. In 1892 Kipling wrote: "And the end of the fight on a tombstone white with the name of the late deceased, and the epitaph drear: 'A Fool lies here who tried to hustle the East.' "

Politics aside, whenever the subject of Ali is raised in my presence, the conversation invariably turns to the man's present pain and suffering. It is at this point that I ask a terrible question: "If you had the opportunity to live one hundred years as a stockbroker or fifty years as Muhammad Ali at the height of his fame and glory, which would you pick?"

Without hesitation, everyone chooses Ali. And so would I, but not simply because of the fame and glory that came his way. I honestly believe that, despite the punishment he received, Muhammad Ali got the best of the deal because he used his wondrous athletic gifts to build a platform from which he could make a difference. When he saw something that was wrong, he stood up and was counted. He spoke and people listened, whether they agreed with him or not.

The bottom line is that Ali never wavered when it came to his convictions, and I grudgingly respect him for that. You could knock the guy down, but you could never knock him out. He was true to himself, his faith, and his friends. He was honest and outspoken, and, in what I believe to be a politically flawed way, he made a difference.

At the pinnacle of his magnificence, he was the greatest athlete of our day, the subject of television specials, books, and magazine and newspaper stories. And during his decline, when the ravages of disease swept through his body, he sought neither our sorrow nor our sympathy. Instead, he greeted us with a smile and a wink, and a kind word. By doing so, he became one of the most memorable human beings of all time.

Despite the debilitating effect of Parkinson's, Ali's smile continues to light the darkest of rooms. The twinkle in his eye retains its magical quality. The advancement of age and disease cannot alter the fact that Ali's very presence at any gathering is so powerful that all else dwindles to insignificance.

The saddest epitaph of all, however, is that were it not for boxing and, yes, the subsequent physical damage he surely received, no one but his closest friends and family would have given a damn whether he lived or died.

Such is fame or the lack of it.

∞∞∞∞∞∞

I was watching the American League playoffs not too long ago with my sons, Terry and Tommy. Although I'm not a big fan of baseball, I could not keep my eyes off Randy Johnson, the Seattle Mariners' star left-handed pitcher. He's about as intimidating a character as I have ever seen in any sport—tall and lanky, hair hanging down his back, and a Fu Manchu–type mustache.

But what really mesmerized me—terrified the crap out of me, really—was the way the Baltimore Orioles' batters dug their heels in at the plate and faced down Johnson. Without so much as blinking—and that takes stones of steel.

Johnson would go into that looping windup of his and—*zap!* That pitch would come screaming in out of nowhere, barely missing the batter, who refused to give an inch. With every pitch, my sphincter would tighten a little bit more. Finally, it having shrunk to the size of a gnat's, I awkwardly shuffled from the room thinking: No way in hell could you get me to stand up there against Johnson with only a bat in my hands. With a rifle, maybe, but not with a small slab of lumber.

I have similar sentiments for other athletes, such as Barry Sanders and Steve Young, who, week in and week out, put life and limb on the line against National Football League defensive linemen and linebackers—oversized guys who are, to my way of thinking, nothing but high-priced bounty hunters.

Correct me if I'm wrong, but isn't the object of football to knock the other guy down as hard as you can? And if he doesn't get up, doesn't that greatly enhance your chances of winning?

I gave up watching televised professional football the day the Washington Redskins' quarterback Joe Theismann's lower leg was snapped in two—repeatedly, thanks to instant replay. Showing the viewers such carnage *once* wasn't enough for the TV executives, who on that day gave new meaning to the term *moral ineptitude* with their continual replays of Theismann's devastating injury.

The point I'm trying to make is that you couldn't pay me enough money to absorb an injury such as Theismann received. Nor could you get me behind the wheel of one of those motorized coffins that NASCAR drivers such as Dale Earnhardt and Geoff Bodine pilot around at speeds in excess of two hundred miles an hour.

Hang-gliding or skydiving? Forget it. Ditto for scuba diving, mountain climbing, or anything to do with motorcycles and guns. And even though I spent much of my youth on the backside of a horse, no way in hell could you get me to actually race one at the track. After all, I once saw Eddie Arcaro take the big fall. I still don't see how he avoided breaking his neck. Jockeys have a death wish, no doubt about it. That's truly one dangerous profession.

But just like Muhammad Ali, I do not see anything wrong with someone stepping through the ring ropes to exchange punches with another boxer. To me, that's no big deal, and I backed up those sentiments on the amateur and professional level for the better part of seven years. The sliced eyebrows, cracked ribs, bruised forehead, busted teeth, and shattered nose cartilage were only part of the physical trauma I was willing to endure in my personal quest for athletic glory.

I also got my brains slapped around quite a bit, but not to any noticeable extent.

Again, that was the price I was willing to pay. The choice was mine, and I made it. It's the same choice a major league baseball player makes, whether he's facing Randy Johnson or not. It's the same choice Sanders and Young, Earnhardt and Bodine make every time they pull on the football pads or climb behind the wheel of a high-powered stock car.

Regardless of the inherent dangers of their given professions, I'm sure they contend that it's no big deal. No matter the athletic endeavor, debilitating injury goes with the territory. It doesn't matter whether you're snow skiing for pleasure or playing football for money. The bottom line is that there are no guarantees you'll make it out in one piece.

Only a damned fool screams for the abolition of professional football when the likes of Joe Theismann or, most recently, Detroit Lions linebacker Reggie Brown sustain a life-threatening or career-ending injury. Every summer it seems as if we're saddened by the death of a Little Leaguer, but no one calls for the dissolu-

tion of organized youth baseball. High school and college football players' die of heat stroke every year, but the grand old game
prevails.

Yet all it takes for an uneducated witch-hunt to scurry out of
control is for one professional boxer to die from an aneurysm.
When such sorrowful accidents happen, a spokesperson from the
medical profession calls a press conference to publicly cast damnation on the boxing profession, and the editorial pages of newspapers nationwide sharpen their mighty pens.

This very thing happened a few years ago when Dr. George
Lundberg, who at the time was the editor of the *Journal of the
American Medical Association,* took boxing to task with the statement: "Boxing is wrong at its base. Boxing, as a throwback to
uncivilized man, should not be sanctioned by any civilized society. . . . Boxing is the only sport in which a person wins by dam-
aging his competitor's brain. That is medically and morally wrong."

I am of the opinion that Dr. Lundberg and others like him, those
who demean a profession without firsthand knowledge, are mentally challenged. While it is easy to talk the talk, it's doubtful they
have ever walked the walk. I suspect these doomsayers would not
know a left hook from a left wing.

The world is full of theorists whose knowledge is built upon the
flimsy foundation of personal bias rather than practical experience.
These individuals will take one tiny fact and paint a broad, all-
condemning picture with it. Such injustice is called a "blanket
indictment," and a morbid example of this was the tragic death of
Princess Diana. Because photographers were chasing the car in
which she was riding, many people believed the subsequent fatal
crash was the media's fault.

Distorting the truth is not that difficult. Government agencies throughout the world have turned disinformation into an art form. The real injustice, however, is how easily the masses are taken in by such scams.

The public's vulnerability to half-truths is what makes con artists so dangerous. These spin-doctors pick up a sports page and read that some unfortunate young fighter has died in the ring. The ensuing reaction is predictable. One man's rectum overrides his brain, and he immediately summons the press to publicly degrade a sport that is as foreign to him as was clemency to Joseph Stalin.

It would be foolish for me to think I could discuss military strategy and tactics with General Colin Powell. I would be an even bigger fool to think I could tell Cal Ripken how to play baseball or Bernard Shaw how to do his CNN telecasts. But I do know boxing. I know what goes into molding a good fighter, what it takes to keep a good boxer at the top of his game, and when it is time to put aside the gloves and walk away from the sport.

My opinions aside, here are the irrefutable facts: The mortality figures published by the *Journal of the American Medical Association* show that there were 335 boxing deaths from 1945 to 1979. This appears to be a helluva lot of fatalities until you discover that the number of deaths in the so-called morally correct sports was far higher during that time span. More people died in motorcycle racing, scuba diving, mountain climbing, hang gliding, skydiving, and horse racing accidents.

While this is a tragic reality of living on the athletic edge, it does not mean that thrill-seeking sports enthusiasts should approach each new day with fear and trembling. Life itself is a gamble. Some people win, others lose; all we can do is take our best shot, which is exactly what Muhammad Ali and so many tens of thousands of others like him have done over the years when stepping through the ropes of a prizefight ring.

∞∞∞∞

The Marine Corps not only taught me how to fight, but how to survive as well. The discipline that enabled me to be a good infantryman also helped me become a pretty good boxer. But more important, I learned in the Marines that boxing was something I wanted to pursue in one way or another even when I left the Corps—something I knew had to happen soon. Although I loved the Corps and everything it stood for, I sure as hell didn't want to be a corporal all my life. But I'd boxed myself in. Because I did not have a college education, becoming a Marine officer was out of the question. As such, there was no way I was going to become Commandant of the Corps. But the Marines had given me the confidence to believe that nothing was beyond my reach, and so I realized it was time to move on and get started on the rest of my life.

I was honorably discharged from the Marines in August 1959 and immediately tried to enroll at the University of Nevada-Reno. I'd read an article in *Sports Illustrated* that praised UNR's boxing program as one of the best in the country, and that, coupled with the knowledge that I would need a college degree in order to succeed, prompted me to head West. Although I did not know exactly what sort of career I wanted to pursue, I did have the desire to continue boxing.

Because of my poor grades at Middlesex, however, I had to take a roundabout route to gain admission to UNR. The first step was summer school at the University of South Carolina, then a semester of study at Armstrong Junior College in Savannah, Georgia. With a well-defined goal in mind, I worked my butt off and stunned the folks back home by becoming a B-plus student. In short order I gained admission to UNR for the winter semester 1960, chose business administration as my major, and subsequently minored in left hooks and the right cross.

Unfortunately, I arrived on the major college boxing scene during its darkest hour. The AMA's crusade against the sport peaked in 1960 when, with the combined might of the nation's college presidents, boxing ceased to be sanctioned by the National Collegiate Athletic Association. The sport's death knell was the result of a fatal aneurysm sustained by Charlie Mohr, a magnificent boxer for the University of Wisconsin, during the NCAA tournament held in Madison, Wisconsin.

Regardless of what you might think of the sport, in no way, shape, or form did collegiate boxing resemble its professional counterpart. We used heavier gloves and wore headgear, which was an innovation first introduced by the NCAA, and we fought three two-minute rounds. As such, we became elite members of what author E. C. Wallenfeldt called "the six-minute fraternity," which was also the title of his 1994 book about NCAA boxing.

Those of us who participated in the sport were far from being street thugs or hoodlums. In fact, when I won the 1960 NCAA welterweight title and the John S. LaRowe trophy as the tournament's most outstanding boxer, I was carrying a B-plus average. I might not have been the brightest student on campus, but I sure as hell wasn't an idiot either. NCAA champions also received an automatic berth into the U.S. Olympic Trials, and it wasn't unusual for some of us to make the team.

I can close my eyes today and still picture Charlie Mohr. He was tall and good-looking and a pleasure to be around. He looked more like a regular student than what you might imagine the typical boxer to look like. He was far from being muscular. In no way did he resemble a rough, tough individual. In fact, he looked like an altar boy, which he was. Had Mohr not lapsed into a coma on the night of April 9, 1960, after losing his bid to win a second consecutive NCAA middleweight title, he would have served Mass at seven o'clock the next morning.

"What's really sad about the accident," said John Walsh, the former Wisconsin coach, "is that Charlie had planned on retiring from boxing after the tournament. He was about two and a half minutes away from never boxing again."

At the time of his death, Mohr, from Merrick, New York, was a twenty-two-year-old senior. He stood about six foot one and was not particularly well built, but damned if he wasn't a great boxer. He was a southpaw who knew how to operate in the ring. He was able to keep orthodox fighters off-balance, and he had a good right jab. Although I don't believe he won many fights by knockout, he sure could box your ears off.

I remember Mohr's quarterfinal and semifinal opponents as being no match for him. But in the finals he fought Stu Bartell, another good fighter from San Jose State. Bartell was a walk-in puncher, a twenty-three-year-old sophomore and a Navy veteran from Brooklyn, New York, who could really bang. He'd fought Mohr twice that season, splitting the decisions, and the Wisconsin

Fieldhouse was overflowing with fifteen thousand fans to watch Mohr defend his middleweight title.

Charlie outclassed Bartell in the first round. It didn't look like Bartell could hit him with a handful of sand, but Bartell kept the pressure on and continued to move forward. In the second round Bartell caught Charlie with a pretty good right hand. I've seen better punches, but this one was a good shot, because Charlie was pulling away when Bartell's punch nailed him high on the forehead. Charlie went down, yet he jumped back up immediately at the count of two. He took the mandatory standing nine-count, then nodded to John O'Donnell, the former U.S. Olympic coach who was refereeing the bout, that he was okay.

O'Donnell waved Bartell out of the neutral corner and Charlie and him mixed it up again. But not for long. Bartell got in a couple more good shots, and when Charlie's legs got wobbly, O'Donnell stopped the fight at 1:49 in the second round. Bartell's hand was raised in victory and the pro-Mohr crowd was momentarily hushed. But then, almost in unison, everyone was on his or her feet applauding what truly had been a good fight.

I remember the Madison Fieldhouse as being a gigantic place, and I was standing in back near my dressing room because I had already completed my fight. I saw Charlie walk back to his corner and sit down on the stool, and I saw him talking to his coach, Vern Woodward. I later found out from Vern that Charlie was apologizing for having lost the fight. Charlie felt as if he had let the school down because his defeat enabled San Jose State to win the team trophy.

After about a minute or so Charlie got up off his stool, slipped through the ropes, and started walking back to the dressing room.

Under any circumstances, that is a long walk. It's even longer when you have been defeated. But it didn't seem to bother Charlie, because he signed autographs all the way back to the locker room.

I remember how bad I felt for Charlie. I also remember thinking that I hoped I would never have to make a walk like that under those circumstances. I watched Charlie step toward the Wisconsin dressing room, then turned away, lost in my own thoughts.

Within minutes, however, the word spread throughout the fieldhouse that Charlie had collapsed. I raced to his dressing room and saw him lying there being worked over by some medical personnel. Charlie's right hand was clutching real hard at one of the medic's arms, and somebody behind me shouted, "Charlie's in bad shape. You've got to get him to a hospital right away."

Everything else is sort of lost in a blur. People were shouting, medics were scrambling around. A stretcher was eventually brought into the room and Charlie was taken away in an ambulance. Shortly thereafter, he lapsed into a coma. He died eight days later, on Easter Sunday.

Because Mohr's family requested that no autopsy be performed, doctors could only speculate that Charlie's death was caused by an aneurysm, a preexisting condition that could have been triggered by a punch. Or something as little as a sneeze.

An aneurysm is a weak spot in a blood vessel that, if subjected to any kind of trauma, can rupture, with the subsequent accumulated blood putting pressure on the brain. Basically, it's a defect that Charlie was born with, and may have ruptured had he simply bumped his head on anything. But it was a punch from Stu Bartell that caused the rupture, and it didn't take any time at all for the pseudointellectuals to unsheathe their theoretical swords.

Because boxing is the antithesis of what academia deems socially acceptable, the public outcry among the nation's college presidents prompted the wholesale elimination of the sport.

In my estimation, that truly was a sad day for mankind. Others felt the same way. One friend of Charlie's went so far as to write a letter to *Sports Illustrated* arguing against the abolition of the boxing program at the University of Wisconsin. As he pointed out, "Charlie loved boxing so much. It had done so much for him, and to ban the sport would be a travesty because boxing had given Charlie so much acceptance, pleasure and notoriety."

Vern Woodward, the Wisconsin coach, worked my corner with Jimmie Olivas at the Olympic Trials held in San Francisco about three months after Charlie's death. Vern loved Charlie like a son, and he also was terribly upset that Wisconsin's faculty had used that tragedy to effectively do away with the boxing program.

"The irony of this sad situation," Vern told me, "is that if Charlie had come back, he'd never have lived in peace knowing that his injury had killed the very sport he loved so much."

While the demise of NCAA boxing had a lasting effect on all of us directly involved with the sport, nothing can compare to the anguish Stu Bartell suffered. Even though Charlie Mohr's father, Charles Sr., wrote a letter to Bartell saying that he neither blamed boxing nor Bartell for his son's death, Stu was never able to completely walk away from the tragedy. He became a prizefighter, but after four professional fights he discovered he no longer had the stomach for it.

"I'd knock a guy down and all I could see was Charlie Mohr lying there," Bartell said. "Charlie's death broke my spirit. It took away my heart."

Charlie Mohr was loved and respected by everyone who knew him. He was the epitome of everything that was good about college boxing—everything that is clean and wholesome about the sport. He was a champion in every respect, and to use his unfortunate accident to do away with a program he and so many others loved so much and from which so many benefited was, in my estimation, downright criminal.

∞∞∞∞∞∞

Charlie Mohr is always with me. Although it's not a conscious effort on my part, whenever I'm around young boxers I can't help but think of him. Charlie was a first-class guy, everything I'd love to see exemplified by my own children—an excellent student and an excellent human being. He had courage and discipline as well as faith—in a religious sense and in his own convictions. He had the remarkable qualities of fairness, trustworthiness, and sincerity. He was as soft-spoken out of the ring as he was aggressive inside. More than anything else, though, Charlie set a good example.

Not too long ago I was invited to a tournament for the Junior Olympics (for ages 12 to 14) held in the Reno National Guard Armory. For the most part, these were young men who did not have much in the way of material things. The group was made up of blacks, Hispanics, Asians, and Anglos—just everyday youngsters, including my own. And standing proudly beside these kids were their parents, who were thankful their children weren't caught up in the insanity other kids that age were involved in.

The young men I saw enter the ring that day were not only in tip-top shape, but they were overflowing with pride—standing tall and majestic in their boxing trunks and shoes, which they bought with their own hard-earned cash. The kids were polite, they were competitive, and they had their attention focused on a goal. They were not dealing crack cocaine to other children. They were not blowing away their parents with shotguns. They were not breaking into the home of an elderly grandmother, robbing her and then beating her to death with a lug wrench. They were not stealing cars and getting caught up in high-speed chases with police officers.

I wish I was making up these scenarios, but I'm not. I see it every day in the courtroom, and it is the saddest commentary on American society that you would ever want to see or hear. Too many of today's youths have no direction, no discipline, no goals or desire. They are too easily swayed by the lure of drugs, theft, extortion, and homicide. Too often they react foolishly, seldom considering the lethal consequences.

My contention is that had these troubled youths been in the boxing ring of that National Guard Armory, they would not have been in our courtroom.

While I'm certainly not naïve enough to think I have all of the answers, give me a juvenile delinquent and two pairs of boxing gloves and I believe I can get that young man's attention. I'm not talking about pounding the crap out of the kid. Working against him in such a fashion would do nothing but magnify his problems. Instead, I'd work *with* him.

I'd place him in a boxing ring and carefully demonstrate that there is no place in society for blind rage and hatred. I'd show him the benefits of self-control and discipline, how a clearheaded, clear-thinking individual can ward off disaster and impending doom through proper physical conditioning. I'd give him a first-hand lesson on the benefits of instruction, repetition, patience, obedience, and restraint.

And in the course of this instruction, that young man would eventually see that it isn't the physical size of the man that's important, it's the size of his heart. He would learn that boxing isn't about irrational aggression or bloodlust; it's about having the confidence and the courage and the physical well-being to meet any and all challenges. It's about never underestimating yourself or others. It's about common courtesy and common sense. It's about self-respect and self-control. It's about discipline of the mind, body, and spirit.

And when the lesson had concluded, I'd sit that young man down and talk to him about setting goals and steadfastly pursuing them. I'd tell him that any idiot can be a follower; it takes a man or woman of high moral conviction and even higher ideals to be a leader. I'd tell him not to follow the example set by a Mike Tyson, but to walk the path blazed by Evander Holyfield and Muhammad Ali. And then I'd tell him about the goodness and graciousness of Charlie Mohr—how precious and fragile life can be, how some very special people are able to have a lasting impact on others, even when their time is up.

These are the lessons being taught to youngsters every day at National Guard armories, gymnasiums, and Boys Clubs from coast to coast. It is instruction imparted by veterans of the ring, men and women whose wisdom is priceless—teachers who know the value of giving an honest effort while being true to themselves and others. And while all of us know that boxing is dangerous, and that everything within our power should be done to make it safer, we also know that the benefits gained from such a discipline far outweigh the risks.

Without boxing I would not have come to grips with or recognized what total discipline is all about. Sure, the Marine Corps instilled a lot of this in me, but it was within the discipline of boxing where I realized that if I wanted to be successful I had to turn it up a notch—run that extra mile of roadwork, go to the gym on those days I did not want to. I had to be prepared to spar a couple of extra rounds when I was spitting cotton and my arms felt like lead. I had to work the heavy and light bags and jump rope when I really wanted to be someplace else—anywhere else.

Instead of slacking off and taking it easy, I stuck to it. And while I have no idea where I'd be today had I quit, I'm sure of where I've been and where I'm going. Believe me, the scenery looks good.

∞∞∞∞∞

Whenever I'm around young men and women, I always ask them if they're hanging around with winners. Invariably I'll receive a glazed look in return, which prompts me to start talking about my favorite subject: how losers are a dime a dozen and that if they hang around losers long enough they'll turn into one.

"Losers are gutless," I tell them. "Losers will quit on themselves as quick as they'll quit on you. Hanging around a loser is contagious. It's a cancer that eats away at your self-respect and self-control. If you don't discover the value of discipline right now, you're in for a sorrowful journey."

If that youngster shrugs, then I know I've lost him. But if I see a light go on within his eyes, then I give him an example of my definition of guts. How, within the span of a month, I refereed two prizefights and saw firsthand two different approaches to life.

The first fighter shall remain anonymous, because I don't wish to embarrass him further. He had crumpled to the canvas after getting hit with a light punch—a punch that I did not believe should have put him down. But I had no choice other than to start the count. When I got to five, he opened one of his eyes and gave me a sheepish look that said, "Hurry up, ref, and count me out so we can both get the hell out of here."

There was no doubt about it: The guy was lying down on the job. He was faking it, taking the easy way out. And that's when I stopped the count and bent down real close to him and said, "Get up off your ass you sorry sonofabitch and fight, or you ain't gonna get paid."

Only then did the gutless bastard get up, but his heart wasn't in it. He merely went through the motions the rest of the way. Chances are he hasn't done anything significant with his life since that embarrassing night.

The second fighter, on the other hand, redefined my idea of courage. The crowd was on its feet, screaming for the knockout, but Tex Cobb was more of a warrior than anyone had imagined. Despite the punishment inflicted upon him by Eddie Gregg, Tex wasn't backing down. Although he did not say so, the expression on his face said: "If I'm gonna lose, I'm gonna lose like a man—exchanging punches with this sonofabitch until he knocks me out."

It was May 20, 1985, in the high desert of Reno, Nevada, and Tex Cobb was giving the fans their money's worth, gamely staying on his feet and slugging it out despite getting the worst of it. For seven rounds, Gregg unloaded on Tex almost at will, connecting with horrific combinations that had the big Texan reeling against the ropes. And now, in the eighth round, Gregg moved in for the coup de grâce.

When Cobb got nailed by a vicious left hook that sent his head spinning, I thought to myself, "C'mon, Tex, go down; you've had enough." But Cobb stayed on his feet and managed to get Gregg into a clinch, thus delaying the inevitable. Then Gregg broke free and nailed Cobb with another left, then a right-left combination that again sent him crashing into the ring ropes. I remember thinking, "What in the hell is keeping Tex on his feet?"

Cobb, now bloodied and battered, shook off the effects of Gregg's beating and landed a few punches of his own. But Gregg went on the offensive again, hitting Cobb with three successive punches and knocking him on his butt. Once Tex got back up on his feet, I stepped in to see how badly he was hurt. The best way to do this is to watch the fighter's eyes to see if they're focused and, if so, what they are focused on. And if you're still in doubt, you ask the fighter: "Are you hurt?" and "Do you know where you're at?"

But Cobb seemed unconcerned about the punishment he'd received. In fact, he paused to spit out a little blood, then began checking out the faces of the crowd sitting at ringside. It was as if he didn't have a care in the world.

I asked Tex if he was hurt, and he grinned at me. The swollen eye would heal, and there was nothing life threatening about his cuts and abrasions. There was no physical reason for me to stop the fight—not as long as Cobb could stay on his feet and defend himself.

But you never really know the extent of possible head injuries. Because I'd rather err on the side of caution, I asked him if he knew where he was. And that's when Cobb chuckled and said, "Mills, I'm in Reno getting the shit kicked out of me."

Dammit, I want people like Tex Cobb on my team.

There's Always One More Fight

The cheers erupted from within the auditorium of the State Building in Reno, Nevada, as I bounced on my toes and waved to the hometown fight fans. I was the invincible badass Marine, the winner of the Corps' All–Far East welterweight title, the NCAA champion who had barely missed making the 1960 Olympic boxing team. I had a 45–4 amateur record, and I was hot stuff.

I remember Bill Dickson, my manager, telling me, "Man, this guy is tailor made for you, Mills. You're gonna start out with a win and everything's gonna be great from here on."

My response to Dickson: "I'm going to eat this sonofabitch alive."

The sonofabitch in question was Artie Cox, a Carson City convict who wasn't supposed to present any particular problems on my climb to the top of the professional welterweight ranks. In those days, the prison system allowed you to fight on the outside. Not that it was of any concern to me. Convicts, cowboys, car salesmen—who cares? Bring 'em on; I'd fight 'em all.

It was April 7, 1961, and I was full of myself, forgetting every hard lesson I had learned in the past five years. Like a damned fool, I was underestimating the enemy as I took my initial step into the ranks of professional boxing.

I remember referee Ted Contri giving the prefight instructions, and I remember hearing the opening bell. But then . . . well, Artie Cox turned out the lights.

I have no idea what crime Cox committed against society that warranted his incarceration, but I wouldn't be surprised if it had something to do with assault and battery. What I have no doubts about is the fact that Cox beat the hell out of me. He rushed me at the bell and dropped me with a right hand that exploded in my face. What followed was lost somewhere in the black hole of semi-consciousness.

Bill Dickson said that when I groggily pulled myself up off the canvas, Cox stepped in and nailed me with a dozen rapid-fire punches to the head, again knocking me on my butt. After the referee counted me out—only thirty-eight seconds into the fight—Dickson said that I sat dazed in a chair in my locker room and kept repeating, over and over, "I can't believe it."

And I couldn't. All I remember is that first right hand thrown by Cox. I saw the punch coming from way back, and yet . . . well, I was helpless—*splat!* I got clobbered, and there wasn't a thing I could do about it. Overconfidence had rendered me incompetent and I had become the biggest of fools—a man who believed his own lies.

Almost nine years later, when I graduated from the University of Utah's College of Law and returned to Reno to take the state's bar exam, I had to sit before a screening panel and answer a bunch of innocuous questions. One of the inquisitors was a gentleman named Clark Guild, a senior lawyer in Reno. He asked, "Mr. Lane, can you pass the bar examination?"

Talk about being nervous. All I could think of to say was, "Ah, Mr. Guild, I don't know. I'm going to try real hard, sir, and . . ."

Guild glared at me and said, "Mr. Lane, the question was, can you pass the bar examination?"

Damn, I didn't know what in the hell he expected me to say, so I opted for the truth. I looked him square in the eye and said, "Mr. Guild, the last time I was certain about anything, they packed me out in thirty-eight seconds. I do not plan to make the same mistake again."

I had, indeed, learned an enduring lesson in the ring. Of greater importance, though, was the fact that I still possessed the mental capacity to act upon it. While there is absolutely nothing wrong with pursuing your dreams, there comes a day when the folly of that pursuit becomes abundantly clear. In boxing, that message, more often than not, is accompanied by a savage beating. Lucky for me that I knew when it was time to walk away from the hard knocks and pursue another career.

Some prizefighters are not as fortunate.

Bobby Chacon won the WBC featherweight title in 1974 with a ninth-round technical knockout of Alfredo Marcano. Eight years later he became the WBC superflyweight champ by winning a fifteen-round decision over Rafael Limon, then lost his bid for the WBA lightweight title on January 14, 1984, via a third-round technical knockout by Ray "Boom Boom" Mancini.

The last time I heard of the forty-six-year-old Chacon, he was collecting soft-drink cans for a living. His diminished mental capacity doesn't allow him to do much else.

Larry Holmes became heavyweight champion of the world on June 9, 1978, when he decisioned Ken Norton. His championship reign lasted seven years, earning him millions. Because he invested his money wisely, Holmes does not have to endure the fight game's agony. But he still does, swinging away at the ripe old age of forty-eight. Last time I looked, he was the eighth-ranked contender, according to the World Boxing Union. The WBU's champion is George Foreman, another enfeebled time-traveler.

Foreman, who also is ranked eighth among World Boxing Council heavyweight contenders, is one of the most likable men I have ever been around. At age forty-eight, he has it all—family, fame, and money. But I would be lying to you if I said I wasn't worried about his well-being. Because he is so addicted to prizefighting's bright lights, I honestly believe he is putting his life in harm's way every time he climbs into the ring. It scares the hell out of me, because George could get killed if he were matched against the wrong fighter—a young pit bull of a boxer; a headhunter, who wouldn't think twice about climbing over Foreman's carcass in quest of riches and glory, no matter how infamously it may be attained.

Sadly, such jackals do lurk on the fringes of prizefighting, reposing in the bleak shadows separating right from wrong.

Jerry Quarry was a magnificent heavyweight, the "Great White Hope" in the eyes of many. Once one of the most popular fighters of his day, he backed down from no one—not Muhammad Ali or Joe Frazier. A two-fisted fighter and a notorious bleeder, he would argue vehemently whenever a well-meaning referee stepped between him and brutal reality, calling a halt to the carnage.

In the latter stages of Quarry's career, rumors abounded of cocaine and alcohol abuse. Today, according to a poignant story written by Steve Wilstein of the Associated Press, Jerry needs assistance dressing himself. His favorite meal is Apple Cinnamon Cheerios. He has slurred speech. He smiles like a child yet shuffles about like an old man. Quarry's neuropsychologist says Jerry now has the brain of an eighty-year-old, that fighting aged him thirty years. He is in the third stage of dementia, which is very similar to Alzheimer's.

Jerry Quarry is fifty-two. Everything he had acquired during his brilliant career has vanished—three wives, $2 million in earnings, $500,000 in savings. He was diagnosed as being in the early stages of dementia in 1983, shortly before recording a first-round knockout of Lupe Guerra. He fought once more, decisioning James Williams, then put aside the gloves and the glory and retired.

Yet enticed by the big-money comebacks of Foreman and Holmes—encouraged by friends who spoke glowingly of impending book and movie deals—on October 20, 1992, Quarry ventured to Aurora, Colorado, a state that does not require a boxing license, and fought a local club fighter, who pummeled Quarry unmercifully for six rounds. For $1,000 in chump change, Jerry's teeth were broken and he sustained cuts over both eyes.

"Jerry is spaced out most of the time," says his older brother James. "He hallucinates. He hears voices. He cries. He gets scared. He gets confused."

James says that his brother now lives in a very, very small world.

〰〰〰〰〰

I turn on the television and I see Livingstone Bramble—Ras-I Alujah, the dreadlocked Rastafarian—getting his brains beat in on ESPN by a young and upcoming fighter. The once-proud former welterweight champion is thirty-seven, a mere shell of his past greatness, and kids who couldn't carry Bramble's jockstrap in his prime are now whacking away at him at will. He has lost eight of his last ten fights.

"Hey, man, I beat Bramble. I beat the champ," these kids tell their friends in the aftermath of these one-sided shams.

Like hell they did. What they pummeled was a faded, forlorn memory.

On February 16, 1985, at the Events Center in Reno, Nevada, Bramble fought one of the greatest fights I have ever witnessed. His opponent that night for the WBA welterweight title was "Boom Boom" Mancini, who had a lot of character but not a lot of natural talent.

I've often made the comment that if you put Marvin Hagler in an alley with Larry Holmes, the odds would be 2 to 1 in Hagler's favor. If you put Hagler against Roberto Duran, it would be even money. But on the night Bramble won that fifteen-round unanimous decision over Mancini, if you had put him into an alley with Hagler it would have been 2 to 1 Bramble. He was as good a fighter that night as I've ever seen.

Not only that, but he showed real class, something you don't see much of these days in the predatory realm of prizefighting.

With about thirty seconds remaining in the fifteenth round, I took Mancini to the doc in order to have a horrible cut he'd suffered over his left eye examined. When the doctor assured me that Mancini could finish the fight, I waved the fighters back into the center of the ring and they went at it again. But Bramble, who had already nailed Mancini with a lot of punches to the face, never hit Mancini on that injured eye again. I thought that showed some class. No purpose would have been served by injuring Mancini further.

Today, Livingstone Bramble is on the receiving end and his opponents show him no mercy. To these younger warriors, he is just a piece of meat.

∞∞∞∞∞

Once upon a time, Iran Barkley was one of the baddest men in the ranks—middleweight, light heavyweight, or cruiserweight. He showed up to fight, and did just that. There was no back down in the guy. Twice he knocked Thomas Hearns unconscious, a rare feat in itself.

Barkley was a heavy puncher with heavy eyes.

The last time I saw him was in 1995. He was broke and washed up. It was enough to make you cry. He had just fought an unknown kid for $250. To earn his keep, Barkley had climbed through the ropes and taken his beating like a man.

That he lost is of little consequence. The real crime is that Barkley's perpetually damaged eyes sustained further damage. The "flesh merchants"—heartless bastards driven by the almighty dollar instead of the best interest of the fighter—could give a shit.

Flesh merchants are uncaring, unconscionable sonsabitches. They are men without principles, without souls. They are so driven by greed that they will subject the fighter to a bout despite the unequivocal knowledge that the fight should not be made.

There is a term in law, fiduciary relationship, which means lawyer to client or trustee to beneficiary. In the realm of prizefighting, this equates to a fighter's manager, trainer, or business agent and the fighter himself. In essence, if you are in contract with that boxer, you have a fiduciary duty to that warrior—you should put your best interests aside on behalf of the best interests of that prizefighter.

The sad fact of professional boxing today is that, more often than not, fiduciary relationship is chiseled away to such an extent that it comes out sounding like "fuck you." And when that happens, good men such as Bobby Chacon, Jerry Quarry, Livingstone Bramble, and Iran Barkley are pushed way beyond their limits of endurance, blinded by their own greed or that of others.

Main Events is a first-class operation run by the Duva family. I have no idea how many prizefighters the Duvas handle, but those under their guidance are dealt with in a most professional manner. For instance, the Duvas have divorced themselves from the usual chicanery of the fight game by making sure each of their fighters has his own accountant and lawyer. As such, the fighters have an extra layer of protection between them and the sharks, those scoundrels whose only purpose in life is to separate the fighter from his money.

Despite these precautions and similar practices by other top-notch promoters, it is amazing how many fighters leave the discipline without so much as a pot to piss in. Then again, because this is a free country, they have the right to be stupid.

As long as I've been in the business, I still cannot accurately explain why fighters are so asinine when it comes to money. I suspect a lot of it has to do with their upbringing, because the vast majority of them come from the lowest of income levels. Not only are they fighting for respect, they are fighting to escape poverty. So, when that big payday does arrive, they celebrate by going nuts. They spend those hard-earned greenbacks as if there were no tomorrow. Which, sadly enough, is too often the case.

Because boxing is a hungry man's business, there always seems to be someone tougher, a younger fighter with far superior skills, waiting to take that prestige away from you. The loss of fame and glory is oftentimes one fight away.

If I were ever to get into the business of managing boxers, I would be the type of manager who would handle that fighter just as I would handle myself. There would be strict discipline all around, in the gym as well as the wallet. I would be up-front with him, and would expect the same in return. We would not do anything behind each other's back.

I would tell the fighter,

> *Listen, son, before we sign this agreement that ensures me of the standard one-third share of your earnings, I want you to fully understand where I'm coming from. I'm going to be making money off your flesh. But what I'm not going to do is screw you out of your fair share. I'm not going to line my pockets at the expense of your blood, sweat, and tears. I'm not going to pad the expense account and I'm not going to charge you for any fictional bullshit services rendered.*

> *But while you're out there getting your nose busted, losing some teeth, and most assuredly sustaining some dementia, I'm going to make sure your tomorrows are taken care of. For example, if you have a big fight coming up and our cut of the purse is going to be $600,000, I will insist that you put aside at least $300,000 and invest it in tax-free municipal bonds. At the going rate of 5½ percent, you'll have $16,500 tax-free to spend each year. It's a start, kid; it's a nest egg. And when those bonds mature, you get the original $300,000 back. And why am I going to insist on this? Because I'm not a flesh merchant; I truly care about you and your future.*

> *I know you are going to make a lot of money, and I know you will want to go out and buy a car. I know you'll want to buy some fancy clothes. There is nothing*

wrong with that. But before you do that, I am going to spell out the monetary realities of life. I will write down exactly how much of your earnings must be set aside to satisfy Uncle Sam, which we'll put aside in the bank. Then I'll give you enough money to piss away as you see fit.

But we're not going to buy a grocery store. And we're not going to buy a tavern or a used car dealership, because those types of investments only pay off as long as you're the champ. Unless you serve the best beer in town or have some sort of gimmick, people will not come around if you're a has-been. You cannot exist on your reputation—scrapbook clippings don't pay the bills. We are going to buy general obligation, tax-free municipal bonds. As long as that state is in existence, that bond is going to be paid. We're going to let your money work for you.

I'll tell them this because nothing is forever. When they walk away from the ring, I want them to be able to enjoy tomorrow—free of debt, free of the punishment they'll surely receive if a flesh merchant comes calling and suckers them with the lure of "just one more big fight." I want my fighter to go out financially set and in one piece. I want him to follow the path of Rocky Marciano, Floyd Patterson, Sugar Ray Leonard, and Marvin Hagler, all of whom hung up the gloves for less perilous pursuits—sound of body, mind, and bank account.

Now, if that fighter agrees to those conditions, then I would gladly become his manager. If he decides that my wisdom is malarkey, then he is free to be stupid. He can do what far too many fighters do: jump blindly into the cesspool and swim with the sharks.

∞∞∞∞

One of the sobering realities of prizefighting is stepping into the ring and seeing the dried blood on the canvas from the previous fight. There is a haunting quality to it. Despite the exhilaration of seeing two magnificent warriors showcasing their talents, despite the cheers from the crowd and the subsequent jubilation of the victorious fighter, I can't help but think, "Jesus, what a way to make a living."

I'm not suggesting that the sight of blood offends me, because it doesn't. What does bother me, though, is the knowledge of what the loser experiences—the absolute emptiness and heartbreak; feeling as if you've let down not only yourself but also everyone who believes in you. There is no easy way to describe defeat. Especially in boxing, where shattered dreams go hand in hand with shattered noses, cuts to your forehead and face, and excruciating headaches from mind-numbing blows to the skull.

Win, and the world rejoices in your corner. You need a calculator to tally the number of friends. Lose, and you suddenly find yourself forsaken. You dwell upon the grief in isolation. You are alone, your aches and anguish your only company.

There have been times when I've seen fighters getting hurt and I'm hurting with them. I've experienced those emotions with Tex Cobb and with Bert Cooper, to name just two.

105

I vividly remember Cooper's gutsy performance against Evander Holyfield on November 23, 1991, at the Omni in Atlanta, Georgia. Cooper, a last-minute replacement for Francesco Damiani, who withdrew after twisting his ankle, wasn't expected to put up much of a challenge. In fact, the media had ridiculed Cooper in the newspapers all week leading up to the fight, pointing out his past problems with narcotics and calling him a bum, a social degenerate, and all sorts of disgusting crap.

But when the bout was under way, Cooper fought the greatest fight of his life. He nailed Holyfield so hard in the early going that the champ crumpled against the ring ropes. Only Holyfield's magnificent heart kept him on his feet. As the fight progressed, however, it became evident that Cooper was out of his league. Between rounds, I found myself thinking, "God almighty, what a terrible position to be in." I felt bad for Bert. He was getting shellacked, as Holyfield seemed to nail him at will.

Admittedly, I was proud of Cooper—damned proud of the obstacles he had overcome and the way he got his ears back and, in light of the slanderous statements made by the media, went out to redeem himself. While he fought a helluva fight, I stopped it in the seventh round.

Of course, quite a few of the fans disagreed with my decision, but they weren't up there in that ring; they did not recognize the damage Cooper was receiving. He could not keep his hands up. His head was being knocked about, his senses were dulled and he was defenseless. But the crowd loved it. Everyone was screaming for more. They couldn't get enough. But I had seen more than I cared to see and called a halt to the bloodshed.

The bottom line is Bert Cooper had given all a man could possibly give. On that night, in my eyes at least, he was a champion—a battered champion. He had earned my admiration.

During a fight I'm all business. My only concerns are that the fighters do their jobs within the framework of the respective rules and that they fight competitively. I'm concerned that the fight is being fought according to protocol, that neither of the fighters is getting hurt unnecessarily. That's what the job entails. My focus is direct. I am worrying *only* about refereeing a good fight. Once things start to get out of hand, once it becomes obvious that one of the fighters has no business being out there, I do not hesitate to call it off. I step in and say, "Son, you've done yourself proud, but that's it—that's enough. There'll be better days."

When the fight has been halted due to a technicality, or when one of the guys has been knocked out, only then do I catch my breath and begin to recognize the cold reality of what I have been a part of. I will look down at the canvas and see all that blood, and that's when you think, "Ah, shit, I know what that poor sonofabitch went through."

I know he is sitting on a stool in his locker room, cold towels wrapped about his neck and head, alone with his suffering, his sorrow.

I remember the night of January 22, 1973, when Joe Frazier fought George Foreman in Jamaica. Don King, Joe's promoter, arrived at the fight in Frazier's car. Afterward, once Frazier had lost on a technical knockout in the second round, King returned to his hotel in Foreman's car. Joe's star had plummeted. He was no longer the champ, no longer the multimillion-dollar meal ticket. More often than not, that's the name of the game.

I have great empathy for the guy who gets beat. The only people standing beside him in the locker room are his real friends. Other than his trainer, nobody else gives a damn about him. The groupies, the bloodsucking hangers-on, have gone down the hall to celebrate with the new champion, the new hero of the moment. That is truly the sick side of boxing, and I refuse to be a part of it.

Whether or not I have worked the fight, I will spend time with the loser. I'll wait for the appropriate moment, wait for him to take off the wraps and come to grips with his defeat, and then I'll tell him, "Son, you have nothing to be ashamed of. You really hung in there, you gave it your all."

The loneliest place in all of sports is the dressing room of a beaten fighter. It is depressing as hell. It's *mano a mano*—just you and your defeat. Your real friends may be there with you. Those who are in it just for the money are long gone.

∞∞∞∞

On August 7, 1962, almost sixteen months after getting knocked out by that Carson City convict Artie Cox, I got another crack at him, this time in Sacramento's Civic Auditorium. He had just been released from the state penitentiary, was as mean as ever, and was telling anyone who would listen that he was going to knock me out in the second round.

By this time I'd smartened up quite a bit. I had won all six of my previous fights, five of them by knockout, and no longer was the overconfident, overbearing sonofabitch I once was. So when

Cox rushed me in the opening round, trying to land that stiff right hand as he had done in our first encounter, I managed to brush aside most of his whirlwind punches. Still, two of them landed—a right cross that shattered every bit of cartilage remaining in my nose, and a left hook that knocked out my bridgework.

With a welt under my right eye, a knot on my forehead, and blood running freely down my face, I spit out the broken tooth and proceeded to beat the hell out of Artie Cox. The first time I dropped him to the canvas was just moments into the second round, leveling him with a left hook to the body. Cox was up at the count of five, but then I dropped him again with a left hook to the gut—*whap!* Cox was up at the count of three. About a minute later, I zeroed in with a left-right combination to the body, and then a left to the head—*thunk!* Down went Cox again, but the bell saved him.

Man, I was on top of the world. This was sweet revenge. It was redemption. For almost sixteen months I had relived the agony of having been knocked out. I had been forced to explain my humiliation over and over to newspaper reporters and friends. But now, by God, I was going to put an end to that subject once and for all.

The third round was a thing of sheer beauty. Cox, a bit glassy-eyed, tried to rush me again, but I sidestepped him and nailed him with a left, a series of right hooks, then unloaded the coup de grâce—a left hook to the pit of his stomach. Down he went with only forty-three seconds gone in the round. Down for good. Say good-night, Artie.

The fans loved the fight so much they showered the ring with coins and dollar bills. It was one of the damnedest things I have ever seen. After we scooped up the money we adjourned to my locker room for a well-deserved celebration; Artie Cox was in his locker room punching his fist through the walls and moaning, "Lane can't beat me; he just can't."

But I had. And in the process I paid a heavy price. I was badly battered and bruised. My nose was history. It would forever remain flattened. Despite the beating I had sustained, my star was on the rise and the boys in the press began predicting sensational things for me. But I knew better.

Regardless of what ringside observers thought, I realized two very important things: I would never be able to beat Emile Griffith, the welterweight champion, and I was getting hit far too often.

I hung around for three more fights, earning enough money to pay for my final year of college. For the record, my last official fight was in Reno against Davie Camacho. I won a ten-round decision against him on February 27, 1963. But three months later, having earned my degree in business administration, I called it quits with a professional record of ten wins and one loss. My manager tried to talk me out of it, but it was, at best, a halfhearted attempt. Bill Dickson was not a flesh merchant. In fact, he was just the opposite.

When you fight in California, two checks are issued: one to the manager, one to the fighter. That way the commission knows the fighter is getting his fair share. During this one bout in Sacramento, I suffered a very bad cut over my eye. In the locker room after the fight, Bill endorsed his check and handed it over to me. "You earned it kid, not me," he said.

Bill Dickson was good people, but like all good managers he wanted me to go out with a big bang. Problem was, I'd had all the big banging I cared to endure. Dickson persisted, though. "You

110

need to take this last fight in Tonopah, Mills," he said. "There's this kid from Las Vegas, a fair fighter, and everyone wants you to fight him for the Nevada welterweight title."

It sounded good, but not good enough. I just shook Bill's hand, wished him the best, and said, "Sorry, buddy, but that's the problem with this goddamn business—there's always just one more fight to make. For me, there is no more. I'm gone. I'm going out under my own power."

I walked away, proud as hell at what I had accomplished in the ring, but even prouder of the fact that I refused to lie to myself . . . well, almost.

In the spring of 1967, just before I entered law school, I picked up the local newspaper and read about an upcoming fight card being held at the Convention Center. I don't know how to explain it any better than simply saying that all of a sudden those pugilistic juices started to bubble to the surface. I found myself bouncing on my toes, bobbing and weaving as I threw punches at an imaginary target. Out of nowhere that combative voice that had been dormant for four long years started whispering to me: "Dammit, Mills, you've gotta go for it. Just one more fight, kid—just one more fight."

I was far from being in perfect shape. I had not sparred, I had not kept up with the necessary work on the heavy and light bags, and I had not been nailed by a punch in almost fifty months. But, on my own volition, I made the fight—the culpability cannot be dumped on my manager, it cannot be laid at the doorstep of some self-serving sonofabitch of a flesh merchant. I was guilty as charged, and, man, did I ever pay the price for my stupidity.

The other fighter was Bobby Knox out of Richmond, California. He was worn and weathered by the wars of the business. For six rounds we beat on each other, toe to toe, punch for punch, blood for blood. And when it was over, my hand was raised in victory.

I went home that night and soaked my throbbing body in a hot tub. My head ached, my arms arched, and my legs ached. Of greater importance, though, my heart ached. I kept reliving that fight, kept seeing Knox's punches coming at my head, kept seeing his face as my own punches impacted into old flesh and bone. And then I drifted off to sleep, dreaming of the man who once was, watching myself age before my very eyes.

When I awoke the next morning, the harsh reality of my own half-truths was abundantly clear. It stared back at me from the bathroom mirror—a brutal, battered reflection of my own simplemindedness. I had seen the enemy, and it was me. I had become everything that I held in contempt, everything I despised. I had become my own flesh merchant.

It was a sobering moment, indeed. And that's when I vowed there would be no more duplicity, no more half-assed comebacks, no more prizefights, no more lies.

There comes a time in everyone's life when they fully realize that they must be true to themselves. This was my day of reckoning. And, by God, I have kept my word.

From Boxing Trunks to Bow Ties

Once I'd graduated from col-
lege and decided it was time to retire from prizefighting, I knew it would be impossible for me to
stay away from boxing altogether. After all, I'd
made a lot of great friends over the years and I
couldn't simply walk away from them or the profession. But my options were limited. I could be a
manager, a trainer, or a referee. Calculating the
amount of time I'd have to devote to the endeavor
and the fact that I now had my sights set on eventually attending law school, refereeing seemed to
be the logical choice.

Because there was no training course for me to
attend—no Refereeing 101, no written exams to

pass—I figured that the same skills that made me a good boxer would also enable me to become a good referee. So, in the fall of 1964, I contacted Jimmie Olivas, my boxing coach at UNR, and asked him if I could officiate some college matches.

"Why not," he said. And just like that, another career was launched.

The only uncertainty I had refereeing on the amateur level was that I was sure some of the opposing coaches would be hesitant at first, wondering whether their fighters would get screwed because of my ties to the University of Nevada. But climbing through the ring ropes and demonstrating that both fighters would get a fair shake proved to be the least of my worries.

It's always been my contention that you need not have been a boxer to be a good referee. It does, however, make you better prepared. Knowing your way around the ring makes the job easier, because you're able to anticipate what the fighters are trying to do—if they're setting up the hook, cutting off the ring, or working on each other inside. You know what to look for. But that knowledge is only as good as your willingness to adapt.

When I was fighting, there was nothing fancy about my style. Because I believe the shortest distance between two points is a straight line, I'd tuck my chin and move straight at the other guy—jabbing, hooking, and unloading the left hand while always moving forward. While there certainly wasn't anything sophisticated about my style, it proved effective. Yet that technique just doesn't cut it when you're officiating. It didn't take me long to learn that I had to be a helluva lot more nimble on my feet as a ref than I'd ever been as a prizefighter.

"You didn't do that bad a job," Jimmie Olivas told me after my refereeing debut, in which I worked seven three-round bouts for the grand total of $10. "Only problem is, you can't be standing around so damned much. You've gotta get the lead out, son. You've gotta move more. You can never move too much."

In truth, I'd been more of a spectator than a referee. I was more intent on watching the overall beauty of what the fighters were doing than focusing on the little things. Instead of continually positioning myself so I'd have a clear view of the action, I got caught up in the drama. Fortunately, my inexperience didn't deprive any of the fighters of a well-deserved win.

I kept working on doing a better job, asking questions and watching how other referees handled themselves, and in short order I conditioned myself to blocking out the application of punching and was able to concentrate on protocol: Is that guy head-butting? Was that a rabbit punch? Is he trying to rub the laces of his gloves against the other guy's face, hoping to open a cut?

But it did take a while for me to feel totally comfortable wearing trousers and a blue dress shirt instead of boxing trunks and gloves. What never left me, though, was the sheer excitement of being in a very special place with very special people.

I don't care if it's a three-round amateur bout or the two best-known heavyweights going at it for the world championship, that contest is the most important fight in the lives of those two boxers. And it doesn't matter if it's being held before a handful of people at some backwater gym in Scranton or in front of twenty thousand fans at the MGM Grand in Vegas. To those involved it is the most electrifying moment of a lifetime. As such, the referee must approach each assignment in a professional manner.

Over the course of the next three decades I would also learn that, on the whole, prizefighting is more aboveboard than not. Yet because professional boxing is a world that most people view only from a safe distance—at best from a ringside seat or from the comfort of their living rooms—the very nature of the brutal business lends itself to misinterpretation. And that is a subject I'll deal with farther on.

As I've said before, I referee because I love the profession. I also get a kick out of the excitement that is generated by a big fight, rubbing elbows with what I consider to be some of the greatest athletes in the world, and being around the profession's insiders—the trainers, cutmen, and managers—most of whom I believe to be outstanding people.

But there's more appeal to the job than glitz and friendship. Refereeing has kept me close to a discipline that has been a major part of my life. At the same time, it gives me the same feeling that I get from being a judge—being in the middle of the action, and sometimes making decisions that may have a lasting effect on people's lives. Some people get a rush out of fixing their car or jumping out of planes—those things don't do anything for me. I get a rush from refereeing a fight. Being an arbiter, whether it's in the courtroom or in a prizefight ring, is what I am. That's where my passion is, and I know of no other way to explain it.

Of course, while the event itself is appealing, the glamour fades quickly. After you've been a small part of so many boxing extravaganzas, you tend not to be affected by the high-profile sportscasters and television cameras, the movie stars and legendary fighters of the past and present. For instance, whenever Evander Holyfield enters a room he's besieged by worshiping fans, most of whom are in awe of his prestige and punching accomplishments. These fans regard Holyfield almost as if he's an idol.

To me, however, Evander is as human as the next guy. He's a good husband and father, a hard-working craftsman, a man of great faith and substance. That he's the heavyweight champion of the world does not matter. Of greater importance is the fact that he's an individual who I'd trust being around my children; a man who not only talks the talk but also walks the walk. And he is not alone in that regard. The same can be said of George Foreman and Alexis Arguello, Sugar Ray Leonard and Marvin Hagler, Muhammad Ali and Danny Lopez. The list goes on and on.

Refereeing's bottom line is that it transcends sports. I believe it's impossible to correctly gauge the outcome of a contest between two evenly matched teams or individuals without good officiating. For example, if an official shows favor by making more calls against one football team than the other, it's impossible for the theoretically best team to win. A referee who is clearly biased, who is not able to function in an unprejudiced manner, is not only flawed but he also flaws the contest. It's criminal. And for that reason alone, sports at all levels need unbiased and equitable men and women arbiters to discern right from wrong. In prizefighting, I refer to men such as Mitch Halpern. People like that get the job done.

Of course, each sport has its outstanding officials—the best of the best. And admittedly, when I first exchanged the trunks and gloves for dress shirt and trousers, my ambition was to be every bit as good as I could possibly be. But I had a helluva lot to learn.

Once I started to feel comfortable about my performance in amateur bouts, I contacted Jim Deskin, at the time the executive director of the Nevada State Athletic Commission, and told him I'd like to referee on the professional level. Again, in short order I was working the preliminary bouts around the state—a couple of four-rounders, then a six and an eight. I just kept working myself up the ladder, proving that I could be trusted with the responsibility. And the more responsible I became, the more fights I was called upon to officiate.

Just like every other endeavor in life, I had to prove myself worthy. I was always asking other referees to critique my performance. In turn, I was told that it was the little things that needed improvement—positioning, moving in quicker to stop the fighters from holding. Others pointed out a major flaw: When you're refereeing big guys, don't move too fast, because it makes them look slow. I took the advice to heart and worked my butt off, because I wanted to do it right. Eventually, the hard work paid off and I finally made it to the main events at Lake Tahoe, where my close friend Sammy Macias and I each earned $12.50 a night plus gas money. Gradually I worked my way up to where I earned $50 for each major fight and $10 for gas.

Of course, no one can make a living from refereeing alone. At best, it's a hobby. During my first five years as a referee, I was employed by the Reno Security National Bank in its loan office, repossessing cars for a living. After I graduated from the University of Utah's College of Law and had passed the Nevada bar exam, I went to work for the Washoe County District Attorney's Office as a trial prosecutor in 1971. The DA at that time was Bob Rose, and he had no problem with me working prizefights in my spare time.

Also working in my favor was the fact that the various boxing people throughout the Southwest and West Coast had given me high marks. According to everything I heard, I'd made a pretty good name for myself—meaning that no one had a bitch against me because I had not screwed up any fights. I just did my job, which

◄ I wasn't always hardheaded and baldheaded. But then again, in 1938 at age one, I didn't know a darned thing about prizefighting.

While I was in Okinawa in 1957, the Corps taught me how to stand on my own two feet. I'm glad they did, because in this fight against the U.S. Army's Sammy Williams I needed all the combat wisdom I could muster. ▼

◄ Here're a few limbs from the Lane family tree: (Back row from left to right) brother Harry; yours truly; my sister Louise; and brother Remer, Jr.: (front row from left) my father, Remer, Sr.; brother Thomas; and my mother, Louise.

◄ The Marines. Here I am in Okinawa with my good buddy, Corporal T. K. Gill. He could guard my flank any day.

The fights were fast and furious in Okinawa. Blame it on the accumulation of punches, but I can't remember the name of the guy I've just sent tumbling to the canvas. ▼

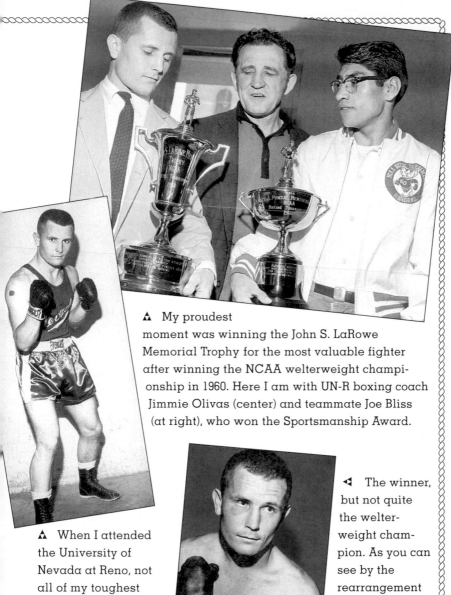

▲ My proudest moment was winning the John S. LaRowe Memorial Trophy for the most valuable fighter after winning the NCAA welterweight championship in 1960. Here I am with UN-R boxing coach Jimmie Olivas (center) and teammate Joe Bliss (at right), who won the Sportsmanship Award.

▲ When I attended the University of Nevada at Reno, not all of my toughest fights were in the academic arena.

◄ The winner, but not quite the welterweight champion. As you can see by the rearrangement of my nose, fighting professionally in 1961 wasn't the easiest thing I've ever done.

The last of the NCAA boxing champions. Collegiate boxing was no longer sanctioned after the 1960 NCAA finals. That's me holding the John S. LaRowe Trophy. ▽

Although his glory was fading, Muhammad Ali still moved like a butterfly when he fought Bob Foster in 1972. ▷

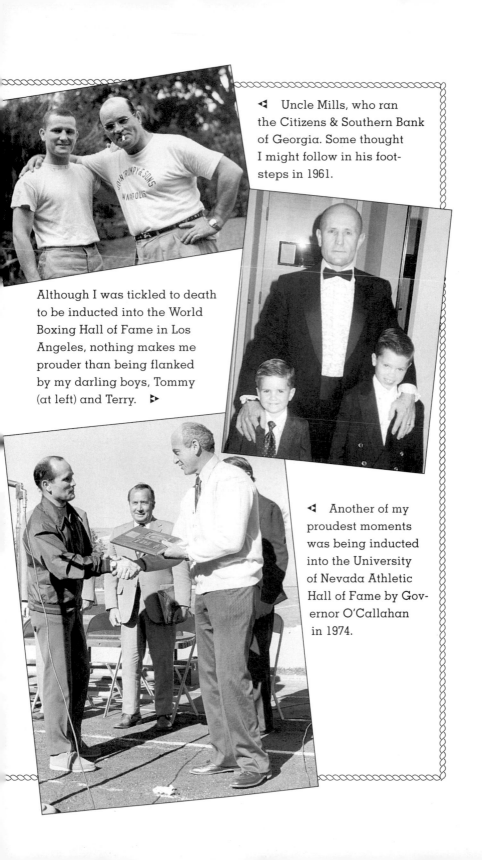

◄ Uncle Mills, who ran the Citizens & Southern Bank of Georgia. Some thought I might follow in his footsteps in 1961.

Although I was tickled to death to be inducted into the World Boxing Hall of Fame in Los Angeles, nothing makes me prouder than being flanked by my darling boys, Tommy (at left) and Terry. ►

◄ Another of my proudest moments was being inducted into the University of Nevada Athletic Hall of Fame by Governor O'Callahan in 1974.

When confronting a
murder suspect, I was
every bit as tenacious
in the courtroom as in
the ring. This was in
1979, when I was a
special investigator
and chief deputy
sheriff working for
Sheriff Bob Galli. ▷

▲ On November 30, 1979, Vito Antuofermo
retained his title in a 15-round draw against Marvin Hagler.

Mike Tyson retained his WBC heavyweight title against challenger Trever Burbick on November 22, 1986. ▷

◁ In 1983 the good people of Washoe County elected me as their district attorney. Shortly after this photo was taken in 1990, the good people elected me to represent them as a district court judge.

I'm the luckiest man on the face of the earth. Here I am with my pride and joys: my wife, Kaye, and our darling sons, Terry and Tommy. ▷

▲ Here I am counting out Juan Roldan in the 4th round after he ran into a flurry of punches from Thomas Hearns, who won the WBC middleweight title on October 29, 1987.

◄ Once he was released from prison, heavyweight contender Mike Tyson had all he could handle from Razor Ruddick, winning a 12-round decision on June 28, 1991.

amounts to keeping the fighters battling within the rules while staying the hell out of the way.

The best compliment I had ever received as a referee was that I was as unobtrusive as a court reporter; I didn't overwhelm the action, I monitored it. And that's exactly the way it's supposed to be. You know you've done a damned good job if, once the fight is over, no one can recall who the referee was.

That would change in the aftermath of my first world championship fight.

∞∞∞∞∞∞

The ultimate refereeing mark of distinction in the 1970s, the wearing of the black bow tie, was reserved for world championship fights only. As such, I made my first fashion statement on November 20, 1971, at Luis Aparicio Stadium in Maracaibo, Venezuela, when I was assigned the Betulio Gonzalez–Erbito Salavarria fight for the World Boxing Council flyweight championship.

Other than it being my first title fight, what makes this event so memorable is that, despite the passage of time, very little has changed in the way some championship fights are conducted outside of the United States. Maracaibo was my first glimpse of how nationalistic fervor coupled with the political realities of prizefighting create a situation in which the playing field isn't even, where "Let's get it on, and may the best man win" is not applicable. It was an introduction I almost did not survive.

Once the Gonzalez-Salavarria fight had been signed, the bout took on nationalistic overtones. Salavarria, who was defending his title, was from the Philippines, while Gonzalez was a homegrown Venezuelan. Holding the fight in Maracaibo did nothing but guarantee ill will. In an effort to mediate the bad blood between nations, Jose Sulaiman, who at the time was the WBC secretary general and in charge of signing the officials, decided that because one of the ringside judges was from the Philippines and the other from Venezuela, it would be best if a neutral referee from the United States worked the fight.

In those days it was common for the referee to score the fight as the third judge, and Sulaiman approached Jim Deskin of the Nevada State Athletic Commission about using a Nevada referee. Sulaiman had no objections when Deskin suggested that I do the fight. I had no problems with it either, especially when Deskin told me I'd be making $500 and would be traveling to South America to earn my keep. I would have flown into the heart of the Vietnam War for such an opportunity.

Once I received permission from district attorney Bob Rose to take a few days off, my grand adventure started to unravel. It began with a telephone call from Deskin, who informed me that there was some difficulty with the WBC obtaining my airline ticket.

"Sulaiman called and was wondering if you could purchase the ticket," Deskin said. "Of course, it won't be coming out of your own pocket. Mr. Sulaiman has assured me that he will reimburse you as soon as you arrive in Maracaibo."

No sweat. I was still young and dumb in the business, and had not yet had any dealings with some of the questionable people who attach themselves to the underbelly of the business. Having so failed the WBC IQ test, I plunked down $300 of my own money for the round-trip ticket to Maracaibo. And so began an escapade that quickly turned into an old Humphrey Bogart movie, complete with Hispanic renditions of Sydney Greenstreet and Peter Lorre.

My flight had a short layover in Miami, and it was there that I was met by Justintino Montano, who was the head of the Filipino delegation, and Rodolfo Narazeo, the Filipino judge.

Montano immediately took me aside and, pausing to nervously look over his shoulder, said, "Señor, we are here to accompany you to Maracaibo."

"Accompany me? Why?" I asked.

"Ah, you do not understand, señor," Montano said in a hushed voice. "These are dangerous times. There are those who do not wish for you to reach Maracaibo."

When I asked who that might be, Montano said, "Ah, señor, it is the Venezuelans. Those people do not wish for you to score this fight. They want you gone. They want a Venezuelan to referee this fight."

I dismissed Montano's theatrics as being nothing more than a veiled threat. Realizing they could not muscle me in that fashion, Montano and Narazeo used a different tack. They tried to play off my sympathy by telling me how good-hearted Salavarria was. I was told that Erbito loved his parents, had never been in trouble, and had nothing but absolute respect for law enforcement personnel. I shrugged off the spiel, despite the fact that Montano and Narazeo kept badgering me, clinging to my elbows as I sought out the airline officials in hopes of alleviating an entirely different matter.

As a state prosecutor, one who had assisted in the long-term incarceration of some heavy hitters, I carry Dr. Colt—a snub-nosed, .38-caliber life insurance policy—with me wherever I go. I've always felt more comfortable with the gun close at hand,

assured of the fact that if any of the low-life sonsabitches I'd successfully prosecuted ever decided to have one of their buddies put
me down, I'd make it as difficult for that assassin as possible.

Because I was an official member of the law enforcement community, the airlines had no problem with me carrying the firearm,
just as long as I surrendered it to the airline captain, who in turn
would return the weapon to me once we landed at Maracaibo. Upon
arriving in Venezuela, I informed their Customs officials about the
sidearm, showed them my credentials, and was breezed through
with no problem at all.

Of course, the ensuing conversation was conducted through an
interpreter, because I don't speak one lick of Spanish. I did, however, understand everyone's smiles. The grins and handshakes from
the Customs' officials conveyed to me that I was not considered a
threat. Within seventy-two hours, however, that interpretation
would be drastically altered.

I checked into my hotel that night, caught a few hours of shut-
eye, then got up and did my normal three miles of roadwork. Later,
after killing a few hours playing tourist, I returned to the hotel and
sat still long enough to be interviewed by a Venezuelan newspaper
reporter, whose English was passable. The guy was friendly enough,
and none of his questions required a great deal of thought. I gave him
the pat answers to the predictable inquiries, yet went out of my way
to clarify that because I had seen neither Salavarria nor Gonzalez
fight, I had no preconceptions as to the outcome of the fight.

Once the reporter was through with me, he sat down with
Rodolfo Narazeo, the Filipino judge. Narazeo screwed up royally
by saying he was familiar with both fighters and had, in fact, seen
them fight the same opponent, a kid named San Sacristan or some-

thing or other. The bottom line is that Narazeo said his boy Salavarria did a better job of whipping San Sacristan than had Gonzalez. Dumb move. Next thing you know, the newspaper hit the streets and the shit hit the fan. The headlines claimed that Narazeo had prejudged the fight.

Despite this, the word on the street was that the fight's promotion wasn't going as well as anticipated and that Salavarria had not received his guarantee, which was in the thousands of dollars. I might be an ol' Georgia country boy, but my mama didn't raise no fool. If Salavarria was getting stiffed, there was nothing to stop me from receiving the same treatment.

As soon I tracked down Sulaiman, I pulled him aside and asked him what the hell was going on. He gave me an innocent smile and said, "Don't worry, Mills. Everything will be okay."

Unconvinced, I said, "Listen, Mr. Sulaiman, I laid out $300 of my own money for a plane ticket. With all due respect, I would like to be reimbursed. Now, as per our agreement."

Sulaiman glared at me.

"Sir," I told him, keeping my temper in check, "the WBC assured Jim Deskin, executive director of the Nevada State Athletic Commission, that I would be reimbursed for that plane ticket as soon as I arrived in Maracaibo. I'm into my own pocket for $300, and all I'm asking for is what's rightfully mine."

I might be mistaken about this, but I don't think anyone had ever had the stones to talk to Sulaiman in this manner before. He started to fidget, then got all huffy and finally reached inside his pants pocket and pulled out a big wad of one-hundred-dollar bills.

"How much was the ticket?" he growled, and I told him three big ones, which he promptly peeled off and handed over.

I then quickly pressed my advantage asking, "What about my fee?"

I thought Sulaiman was going to have a heart attack. His eyes got real big and his face turned bright red. But obviously realizing he could not intimidate me, he peeled off five more big ones and handed them over, then pivoted on his heel and disappeared in a cloud of smoke.

Of course, I wasn't the only one having difficulty with Sulaiman and the WBC. A few days prior to the fight, I sat in on the usual rules meeting with the other fight officials and was amazed that it degenerated into a full-blown, four-hour bitch session. The Filipino delegation claimed it was somehow getting screwed. Before you knew it, Justintino Montano, the head of the Filipino delegation, got into a squabble with one of the members of the Venezuelan delegation. Then Sulaiman jumped up and tried to mediate the argument, which quickly turned into a pissing match between him and Montano.

It was the damnedest thing, a virtual circus that did nothing but enhance my apprehensions about the fight. Nothing was going right. The natives were getting restless, and the people supposedly in charge were acting like damn fools.

I put my foreboding on the back burner, however, the night of the fight. I was too excited. Besides, I thought I looked awfully darned spiffy wearing my new black bow tie.

The fight itself was everything I figured it would be. Salavarria and Gonzalez got in each other's face, unloading a flurry of jabs, hooks, and hard right hands. Both were in excellent physical condition, and battled straight from the heart. As prizefights go, this one was truly magnificent. It was fifteen rounds of nonstop action, and they flat-out worked my butt off. Despite my being in great shape, the combination of their unrelentless fighting coupled with the heat and humidity took its toll. There were moments in the ninth and tenth rounds when I actually got a bit woozy.

But nothing seemed to bother Salavarria or Gonzalez. They pounded on each other without letup—jabbing and feinting, then landing combinations one after another. It truly was one helluva fight, and a close one at that. The fifteenth round was just as brutal as the first, and the fight ended with a flourish from both kids.

In Venezuela, the scorecards were not turned in until the end of the fight. In the United States, the scorecards are handed over after each round, which eliminates the possibility of fraud—one of the three officials doctoring his scorecard as the fight progresses.

Even though the fight was close, I scored it 147–146 in favor of Salavarria. That was what I wrote on my scorecard, and then handed it over to one of the Venezuelan officials at ringside.

As I joined the fighters in the center of the ring, the crowd's chants for their man Gonzalez grew louder and louder. There was a momentary silence as the ring announcer bellowed into the microphone: *"Señoras y señores . . ."* And then the decision was announced—in Spanish, as expected. But what I had not counted on was the confusion inside the ring.

The dejection on the faces of Gonzalez's cornermen and the fans at ringside was unmistakable—their man had lost. Of course, knowing how the nationalistic fight game was always played, I knew that Emilio Lugo, the Venezuelan judge, had surely voted for Gonzalez. And I knew that Rodolfo Narazeo, the Filipino judge, had surely voted on behalf of his man Salavarria.

So the deciding vote had been mine, and I had scored it 147–146 for Salavarria.

Without the least bit of hesitation, I gritted my teeth and raised Salavarria's hand. And then all hell broke loose. First, Gonzalez's manager rushed at me, his fists clenched in a fighting stance, and screamed: "You're loco. Betulio won." And then everyone else in the Venezuelan contingent started screaming at me, including the ring announcer, so I dropped Salavarria's hand and raised Gonzalez's hand instead.

Of course, then the crowd started cheering and singing and having themselves a grand old time, happy as hell. But then Salavarria's people went nuts on me, yelling: "No, no. It was a draw!"

Talk about a raft of snakes and bats. I remember thinking, "Draw? How can it be a draw?" But faced with the dilemma of the inmates running the asylum, I raised both fighters' hands.

And that's when the riot erupted.

I spent a few anxious moments ducking bottles and chairs that were tossed into the ring, wondering how long it was going to take before I died. I moved out of the line of fire and toward one of the corners, but then some jerk at ringside started pounding on my legs. I stepped aside, only to encounter another irate fan who had climbed through the ropes and jumped right into my face. I squared off to drop the beady-eyed sonofabitch, but it dawned on me that he wasn't alone—there were a whole bunch of his buddies out there who'd also like a piece of me. So, discretion being the better part of valor, I slipped his punch and ducked back into the center of the ring, intent on finding a big police officer to hide behind. Or a small one for that matter.

The stadium was absolute chaos. Everyone seemed to be pressing in on us at ringside, screaming and yelling a bunch of undecipherable gibberish. But I got their drift. I was a prime candidate for a lynching.

And then, out of nowhere, the police stormed into the stadium, wielding their nightsticks as they clubbed their way into the ring. The cops escorted the Salavarria contingent to safety. Shortly thereafter, National Guard soldiers fought their way through the gauntlet and escorted the Filipino judge out of harm's way. I was left to fend for myself, with nothing but two medium-sized police officers to stem the onrushing tide of every nut case in South America. But damned if those cops weren't magnificent, beating off a couple of lunatics who had managed to jump into the ring.

Moments later, the soldiers returned to save the day. While at least forty of them made a corridor for me through the crowd, two others grabbed hold of me and literally lifted me out of the ring and through the horde of crazed fans. Someone spit on me, then someone else punched me in the face. By this time I was numb with terror, which is why the punch didn't hurt as bad as it normally would have. The soldiers maneuvered through the crowd, flaying away with their nightsticks as they fought their way through the infield and into a tunnel, and finally toward the safety of a concrete holding room beneath the grandstands.

As more insane fans pressed in on us, the soldiers countered with one last flurry of their nightsticks. And then a door opened and I was shoved into a bleak room with six guards as company. Once the door was bolted, I collapsed in exhaustion—alive, but only because of the quick and efficient work from the Maracaibo police and the Venezuelan National Guard.

After letting me cool my heels in that concrete room for about half an hour, the cops returned and again escorted me through the hostile crowd to a getaway car, which took me back to my hotel. Just like in those spy movies, I left my belongings at that hotel, ducked out the back entrance, and was whisked away to yet another hotel. Once there, I locked myself in my room and knocked off a couple of beers.

I was working on the second brew when a WBC official telephoned. "Mr. Lane, we wish for you to remain calm," he said. "Everything has been arranged. We have taken care of your airline reservations. You'll be leaving tomorrow."

"Tomorrow? Why not tonight?" I screamed at him, but he had already disconnected the line.

Next day at the airport, thinking the worst was behind me, I was jerked out of line at Customs and roughly escorted to yet another concrete holding room where five of the meanest-looking *federales* took turns shouting and screaming at me. As expected, it was a one-sided interrogation, because I had no idea what they were babbling about. There was no mistaking the pissed-off expressions on their faces, however.

Finally, in exasperation, I asked, "So what's the problem now?"

One of the cops gave me a tight smile, thrust my gun into my face, and started yelling at me again. Lost somewhere in the no-man's-land of our language barrier, these guys obviously thought I had brought my firearm into their country illegally. I tried as best I could to talk my way out of the problem, but no one could understand my explanation. Or if they could, they weren't buying my story. The only thing that was abundantly clear to them was my identity. I was the evil gringo referee who had tried to screw their fighter. Once again, I felt as if I would never get out of Maracaibo alive.

Finally, an English-speaking officer entered the room, and I was able to explain the situation to him—how, as a law enforcement official myself, I had obtained permission to bring the firearm into Venezuela. He, in turn, explained the situation to everyone else. Heads nodded, but those irate expressions did not go away. After another half-hour of haggling, I was allowed my freedom, but without my gun. Because I was in no position to argue, I made a hasty retreat to the airplane.

As the plane zoomed down that runway and into the air, the thought in my mind was "Happiness is Maracaibo in your rearview mirror."

Within the safety of the plane, sitting at thirty thousand feet somewhere over the Caribbean Sea, the gentleman sitting next to me recognized who I was and attempted to explain the insanity of the night before. As he pointed out, "You are not in the United States, Mr. Lane. You have to remember, it is their country—their laws, their rules."

"Yeah," I told him, "but what about good sportsmanship?"

The gentleman, who owned a company in Venezuela, smiled and said, "In Latin American countries one does not say 'I dropped it.' Instead, you say 'I let it drop' or 'It fell.' There is a subtle difference. For instance, if I discover that someone in my plant is stealing from me, I have two choices: fire him or forget it. In Latin America, you never confront an individual and accuse him or her of being a thief. To do so is to insult their dignity, their pride."

In essence, regardless of what the correct decision of the Gonzalez-Salavarria fight might be, once I had raised Salavarria's hand I had injured the pride of all Venezuelans. In the ensuing confusion, when I also had raised Gonzalez's hand, all I accomplished was to add insult to that injury. I was damned if I did and damned if I didn't.

But what the hell. I was just damned glad to get out of Venezuela in one piece.

It wasn't until I landed back in the States that I learned the full extent of the chicanery I had been an unwilling partner to. Bear with me, though, because the scenario is still confusing as hell. It began with the ring announcer, who related the verdicts as such: "Judge Rodolfo Narazeo of the Philippines scores it 148–147, Salavarria. Judge Emilio Lugo of Venezuela scores it 146–146, a draw . . . whoops, sorry. Lugo scores it 147–145, Gonzalez. And referee Mills Lane of the United States of America scores it 147–147, a draw."

Somewhere amid all of that bullshit, the riot started. I will never know what truly happened because once I turned in my scorecard I never saw it again, but I had voted for Salavarria, and you can bet the Philippino judge voted for Salavarria, while the Venezuelan judge voted for Gonzalez. The bottom line is Erbito Salavarria won the fight fair and square. However, there was nothing fair or square about this fight. Ramon Barrios, president of the Maracaibo Boxing Commission, jumped into the ring moments after the rioting began and announced to the crowd that their boy Gonzalez was declared the winner because of doctored water. He said that Salavarria had used an illegal substance—sugar—in the water at his corner.

Not to be outdone, Jose Sulaiman went on record the following day, lending his support to the Venezuelan conspiracy theory by stating, "Salavarria drank the treated water. There are many witnesses to prove it. This was a violation of the rules of the fight. That is why the local boxing commission declared the Venezuelan the new champion."

Sulaiman heightened the intrigue, however, by stipulating that the doctored water "was a mixture of something more than sugar and water. The mixture must now be analyzed thoroughly. The results will be taken to the WBC."

It was seven years before I was allowed to work another championship fight.

Finally, in April 1978, the Nevada State Athletic Commission assigned me the Larry Holmes–Ken Norton bout for the WBC heavyweight title. Although Sulaiman put up a big stink, much to his credit he approached me after that bout and said I did a very commendable job. Ever since, he has never complained about me being assigned to one of his fights.

As for that handgun left behind at the Maracaibo airport? As soon as I was safely back at the Reno DA's office, I made a few telephone calls. A friend of mine in the courthouse had a sister in Washington, D.C., who in turn contacted our ambassador to Venezuela. I don't know what this guy said to those Maracaibo police officials, but my weapon was returned to me through diplomatic channels.

Getting Your Ears Back

Underachievers disgust me. I have absolutely no tolerance for those individuals blessed with an abundance of talent who end up squandering their gifts because they're just too damned lazy to attend to business.

Despite the fact he was a world champion, I believe Hector "Macho" Camacho was an underachiever. He had great talent but never really maximized it, didn't do everything he could with it. The same can be said for Donald Curry. When he knocked out Milton McCrory on December 6, 1985, I believe on that night he was one of the greatest-looking fighters I'd ever seen. Maybe the greatest fighter at that time at any weight in the world. Weighing in at 147 pounds, Curry became the undisputed welterweight champion. But about five months later he weighed 162. "What the hell's wrong with you?" I asked him. "Here you are a world champion and you're abusing your body. That's wrong, damnit."

I'm sure Curry didn't want to hear that, but it was the truth. Here was a guy with all of that God-given talent and he was just pissing it away. He was cheating himself, abusing his tools. No self-respecting carpenter leaves his hammer and saw out in the rain. That would be stupid, and there are some things you just don't do, not if you have pride in what you're trying to accomplish.

But there are some people you just can't get through to, no matter how much you reprimand them. Roberto Duran, for instance, is one of the saddest examples of this that I've ever seen. From bell to bell, over a period of time, Duran was probably the greatest pure fighter I ever saw. He had speed, knew how to use the ring to his advantage, and possessed devastating punching power with either hand. On top of that, he was a stone-cold personality. Whenever I looked into his eyes, I saw nothing there— no compassion, no remorse at all. It was like looking into the eyes of a shark.

Roberto Duran could easily have been known as the greatest fighter of all time, even greater than Muhammad Ali. But Duran abused his tools. Late in his career, he weighed 190 between fights, which is downright criminal for an athlete of his caliber.

Underachieving isn't only confined to boxing, though. The quickest way for a lawyer to get in my doghouse is to skulk into the courtroom and request that a trial be postponed because he or she is not quite prepared. That sends me right through the roof. Inaction is not the defining principle of our judicial system. And it most certainly should not be the criteria by which a person's life is lived.

Yet more often than not it seems as if we have become a nation of excuse makers. The job doesn't get done because it's raining, it's too hot, or some other bullshit. It seems as if we spend more time concocting excuses for our many failures than we do attending to the business of successfully completing the task at hand. We exhaust ourselves figuring out whom to blame rather than figuring out how to solve the damn problem.

When I was boxing, if I found out my opponent was running two miles each day, then I'd run three. No matter what it took, I was going to be better prepared. That's the key to being a winner.

Because I always had to work extra hard to get the job done, whether it was preparing for a fight or studying long into the night to fully understand the nuances of a legal brief, I know that if something needs to be done, then, by God, it can be done. As I've said before, all you've got to do is get your ears back and do it. I'm not interested in hearing your excuses. I don't want to hear what you can't do. I want to know what you *can* do.

My disgust for underachieving is rooted in my childhood; I was a perfect example of unintelligent inaction. While my father could find no fault with my physical labors in the hay fields, he had reason to be critical of my efforts in the classroom. I wasn't trying hard enough. I wasn't doing what it took to get the job done.

My response was always the same: "Daddy, I am working hard. I am trying."

Of course, I was not applying myself as arduously as I was capable of, but I did not realize it at the time. I was occupied with far more important matters. Would the Lone Ranger and Tonto prevent that evil gang of cutthroats from stealing everyone's farms? Could Billy Conn stop Joe Louis?

While I have always possessed average intelligence and average skills, my youth is best defined by the fact that I also suffered from below-average desire. In an attempt to remedy this problem, in the fall of 1950 I was sent to a boarding school called Middlesex in Concord, Massachusetts. My father had attended the all-male enclave as a child and he had nothing but praise for the institution. It was one of those "If it was good enough for me, it's good enough for you" situations in which a young man of twelve has no say. My father wanted to give me the finest preparatory education possible, and there was no arguing his decision.

I will never forget the moment when my parents left me. Daddy said, "Son, it's time for us to say good-bye." I was trying my best to be a man, even though I was scared to death, and I remember crying as my mother and father got into the car. I can close my eyes even now and still see them driving down that small asphalt road, on their way back home without me.

Yet as traumatic as that experience was, I learned an invaluable life lesson from it. Even though you do not know how in the hell you are going to get through what appears to be a catastrophic situation, you somehow do. Although you don't realize it at the time, you are able to survive because you end up reaching deep down inside yourself and getting acquainted with courage.

Nonetheless, Middlesex was a bitch. I hated the place. I didn't like having to wear a coat and tie all the time. I didn't like the discipline. I didn't like some of the teachers, who were called masters, and I disliked schoolwork in any form or fashion. And being stuck near the top of the eastern seaboard was like being stranded on the moon. I was told when to go to sleep, when to wake up, when to eat, and when to study. Throughout my first five years there, I even had to wait on tables in the dining hall.

Athletics was the only thing that made life bearable and I participated in every sport I could. In fact, that was the first time I ever competed in anything. It was pretty neat, because we had real uniforms, helmets, and pads. It was fun, even though I was a little itty-bitty boy of about four foot eleven. While I lettered in crew and baseball, my favorites were football and ice hockey. Both provided the physical contact I was attracted to, even as a youngster.

I was a linebacker on the football squad, and flat-out loved hitting people. I'd be lying if I didn't say that it was fun knocking guys flat on their butts. Hockey was a bit different because, never having seen ice before, I did not know how to skate. The first time I laced on the skates, I hit the ice and landed smack on my butt. I got up, fell down, and got up again. Next thing you know, the coach brought out a little wooden chair and I pushed it in front of me as I got my bearings. I eventually graduated from a chair to a hockey stick.

Because I wasn't a great skater they made me the goalie. In those days, goalies didn't wear masks, and I managed to get my fair share of bumps and bruises. I even got knocked unconscious once when I got nailed in the mouth by the puck. That's how I first broke my tooth. The dentist ended up taking the nerve out and capped the tooth, but I got it knocked out again the following football season. It was worth it, though. Getting my lights turned out was still more fun than having to hit the books.

I survived Middlesex by taking it one day at a time. It was like climbing a mountain. The last thing you want to do is look up at the top, because when you realize how far you still have to go, there is the tendency to quit. I got through the experience by climbing from one rock to another, moving up a little bit at a time. It was day to day, class to class.

That's also how I survived Marine Corps boot camp. I was forced to dig down deep inside myself for courage, taking hold of it and turning what some might think of as a bad situation into a good one.

The Corps was my line of demarcation. I was given a choice between being a gutless, lazy sonofabitch, or being a man's man. The choice was easy. I was forced to grow up, and in the process I became convinced that he who lives without discipline dies without dignity. I learned how to fight through the pain in order to get the job done. I learned that no job was undignified if done with dignity. I learned how to take care of business, whether it was cooking my own meals or washing my own clothes or picking up after myself.

More than anything else, though, the Marines taught me what leadership was all about. Of course, you never really grasp the principle until you've had the misfortune of being led by an asshole. I had one sergeant in particular who corrupted authority. If I saw him today, I'd jump in his face and say, "Okay, brother, you and me are going outside." I'd kick his ass in a heartbeat.

This sergeant led by intimidation. He was a shit-bird, which is the worst insult you can give a Marine. When payday came and he had money, everyone got liberty. When he ran out of money, everybody had field day. We stayed in our barracks and cleaned it from bulkhead to bulkhead. This guy was a no-good sonofabitch. I despised him and anyone else who bullies someone simply because they have the authority to do so. That holds true to this very day.

Leadership is not yelling and screaming at someone because he or she makes a mistake. Leadership is not pissing and moaning every time something doesn't go your way. Leadership is *never* asking someone to do a task that you are unwilling to do yourself. If I have the authority to command or order someone to do something, they'll do it willingly because they'll know I have the stones to do the job myself. It doesn't take guts to do something if you're not afraid to do it.

There's a story that epitomizes everything I learned in the Corps, one that I once heard about the ParaMarines. Because the Corps didn't have a paratrooper training facility at its disposal, the Marine colonel who was to command the unit asked permission of the general at Fort Benning, Georgia, to use the Army's.

"No problem," the general said. "How long will you and your men be here?"

"How long will it take you to train my men how to fold a parachute?" the Marine colonel responded.

"Hell," the general said, "I can teach you how to do that in a couple of hours. But that's not how the training works. We'll have to teach your men how to jump from the respective towers, how to roll on impact so they won't break a leg or an ankle. We're talking about several weeks."

The Marine colonel said, "Begging your pardon, sir, but all I will need is half a day. All the training my men will need is how to properly fold a parachute."

Of course, the Army general was flabbergasted. He said, "Okay, but once you get your men up in that plane and over the target area, how in hell are you going to get them to jump out?"

"I'll order them out," said the Marine colonel. "When I say jump, they'll jump, because they know I'll be jumping right along-side them."

The Marine Corps first taught me how to crawl, then how to walk like a man. And when properly led, I would fight my way into hell itself. I would make that terrifying journey because I'd know the officers leading the way and the NCOs on my flanks would ensure my survival.

When I was discharged from the Corps in 1959, I no longer doubted myself. I was so confident of my ability to succeed that the only thing I feared was fear itself. No longer willing to accept mediocrity, I had my feet firmly planted on a ground of my own choosing. Because I *wanted* to enroll at the University of Nevada-Reno instead of being told that was where I would attend school, because I *wanted* to go to law school and become a lawyer, a district attorney, and eventually a judge, I worked as I had never worked before.

The young man who was satisfied with a C-plus at Middlesex was long gone, replaced by a hard-nosed Leatherneck who was disciplined to such a degree that average work was unacceptable. As such, I was a B-plus student at UN-R. My goals were established and I fought my way through the grind of academia.

My IQ had not increased one bit in the four-year gap between my senior year at Middlesex and my freshman year at UN-R. What had changed was my attitude toward life. I came to believe that no task was impossible. I was of the opinion that the sorry phrase "I can't do it" no longer existed in my limited vocabulary.

I hated schoolwork just as much at the University of Nevada-Reno as I had at Middlesex. But I endured, because I had a goal and *nothing* was going to stop me from reaching it. That book, that inane course in physics or geology, was no different from anyone I'd fought in the ring. Instead of keeping my hands up, my chin tucked, and moving forward, I kept my dreams held high and my brain focused, and I moved upward and onward.

Because I'd learned that you can't lead others until you've learned to properly lead yourself, I continued to inch closer to being all I could possibly be. Although it proved to be an ongoing process, it wasn't impossible because I continued to follow the examples set by individuals who had earned my total respect. Men such as Rocky Marciano, Willie Pep, Sugar Ray Robinson, and Archie Moore—magnificent fighters, one and all. Men gifted with speed and power, class and magnetism.

Whenever they entered the ring, the world watched in wonder. It seemed as if they could do no wrong. Our troubles no longer seemed that important, because if Marciano and Moore or Pep and Robinson could surmount all barriers, then by God so could we. In a modern context, I'm referring to men such as Muhammad Ali and Ray Leonard and Marvin Hagler. On the whole, they were true warriors who maximized their brilliant talents and unflinchingly charged head-on toward their goal. Nothing was going to stand in their way. They fought through the daily aches and pains, through the trauma of disappointment and failure of life, and eventually succeeded, no matter the obstacle.

In the spring of 1996, I honestly believed that Riddick Bowe was in this category. I'd seen all three of his fights against Evander Holyfield, the first two of which were as good as any in recent memory, and I considered Bowe to be the best of the heavyweights. His tools were far better than Evander Holyfield, and at least one notch above Mike Tyson.

Bowe had it all—size, strength, an impressive chin, and devastating punching ability. Although he couldn't knock you dead, he did have a good jab, a better than average right hand, and a decent hook, and he knew how to handle himself on the inside.

Despite these impressive credentials, though, Riddick Bowe did not maximize his capabilities. He would not pay the price to be the best. Although I liked the guy, he was, in my mind, a failure because he didn't go as far as he could.

Evander Holyfield, on the other hand, has more heart than anyone. I worked the fight when he won the cruiserweight title from Carlos DeLeon in Las Vegas on April 9, 1988. Holyfield's trainers had their hands full getting him to make the 195-pound limit. The first time he hit the scales, he weighed 196. They walked him around a bit, then he weighed 195½. Holyfield's trainers had to put him on the scales three more times before he finally hit 195 on the nose. And then he went out and fought a great fight against DeLeon.

Holyfield was hurting—having to shed pounds he should not have been forced to shed weakened him. Yet he rose above it and fought a truly magnificent fight. He had it all going for him that night. In fact, that's the best I've ever seen him.

Afterward, I listened to what Evander had to say to the press. Normally, what you hear in these sessions is the usual street jive and back-alley nonsense about being the baddest cat in town. With Holyfield, though, the message was entirely different. First, he praised DeLeon. And then, instead of tooting his own horn, he spoke of his faith. Granted, everything he said was steeped in religion. But the manner in which he conveyed his convictions was sincere, right from the heart. He was so humble that I found it impossible to find fault with him.

I remember someone asking Holyfield about anger, and he said, "Like the Bible says, you've got to be able to control your anger. It's an asset to control your emotions and not allow the devil to take control. It's harder living for Christ than it is living for the devil. Live for the devil and all you have to do is sit back, relax, and enjoy it. I don't deny that I am a Christian, but it's no good to brag about it. The Bible says, 'The light should shine so that people would know you without even asking.' I believe that."

Holyfield was absolutely incredible—a fighter spouting off like an evangelist. I was impressed. Once the media had its fill, I chatted with Evander for a while and asked what his ambitions were. Without hesitation he said, "I'm going to be the heavyweight champion of the world."

I'm no dummy. I knew that Mike Tyson was, without doubt, the baddest man on the face of the planet. Mike ruled a division filled with contenders in name only. Yet here was this unknown entity, Evander Holyfield, a bright-eyed, Bible-quoting cruiserweight with the biggest heart I've ever seen, making as bold a statement as I'd ever heard, one that most boxing insiders would consider to be blasphemous.

But then again, I had just watched him fight as great a fight as you would ever want to see and now I was looking him square in the eye. What I saw was a superior being with total commitment and an absolute belief in his convictions. I know it sounds crazy, but I thought he had a shot.

Next thing I knew, Holyfield ran up the score, dropping James Tillis, Pinklon Thomas, Michael Dokes, Adilson Rodrigues, and Alex Stewart. He fought through fatigue, he fought through disparaging comments from Tyson and his promoter, Don King. In the meantime, Tyson had his lights turned out by James "Buster" Douglas in Tokyo. And then Holyfield turned out Douglas's lights at the Mirage in Las Vegas on October 25, 1990, exactly thirty-two months and sixteen days from the moment he said he would become the heavyweight champion of the world. Now that's what I call perseverance.

Twenty-five months later, Evander would lose the title to Riddick Bowe. One year later, he would decision Bowe to win back the title, only to lose it again five months down the road to Michael Moorer. Yet throughout these trials and tribulations, Evander Holyfield endured despite ridicule from the media for being a "washed-up has-been," despite calls from the medical profession and knowledgeable boxing insiders, including myself, that to continue fighting would be to guarantee pugilistic dementia.

I refereed the fight in Atlanta, Georgia, in 1991 when Holyfield was forced to call upon every ounce of courage he possessed to eventually defeat Bert Cooper via a technical knockout. What bothered me the most about that fight was the fact that Evander was getting hit too often and too hard by Cooper, a journeyman fighter at best. If I had been Holyfield's manager, I would have pulled him aside after that fight and said, "Listen, son, you have all the money you need. You've conquered all the horizons you've wanted to conquer by becoming the undefeated heavyweight champion. It's time to hang it up. You need to walk away from the business, and you need to do it *now.*"

But Evander refused to quit on himself. Almost thirty months after the Cooper fight, I refereed the Holyfield-Moorer bout, which was Evander at his lowest ebb. He appeared to be en route to an easy victory after knocking Moorer to the canvas in the second round, but then everything went south. All of a sudden, Holyfield was confused and out of synch. He struggled to throw punches and his defense against Moorer's right jab was almost nonexistent. Evander would get nailed, then take a couple of steps back and frown. It was almost as if he didn't know where he was.

I'm not being overly dramatic when I say that I suspected he might be suffering the initial effects of pugilistic dementia. I felt so strong about this that I approached Shelly Finkel, Evander's manager, after the fight and said, "Get him out, Shelly—get him out *now.* Something's not right with him."

I believe Finkel had the same suspicions, because he turned to me and said, "Don't worry, Mills. We'll retire him."

It never happened. As it turned out, Evander had not fully recovered from his previous bout with Bowe and was suffering severe pain in his left shoulder, which prevented him from either going on the attack or curtailing Moorer's right-handed onslaught. Holyfield's problems escalated after the fight when he suffered a severe case of dehydration. Then, when properly hydrated, he was given morphine for his injured shoulder at a Las Vegas hospital, and complications set in. Holyfield was subsequently misdiagnosed as having a heart condition—a noncompliant left ventricle.

What all of us so-called hotshot boxing experts thought was a bad heart turned out to be nothing more than a bad case of fatigue coupled with the usual aches and pains associated with prize-fighting.

When Holyfield later claimed to have been healed by evangelist Benny Hinn, people scoffed. When he passed a series of medical tests at the Mayo Clinic, people shook their heads in disbelief. And once he was relicensed and started reestablishing himself in the ring, people sat back and told themselves: "Yeah, well, he might look okay against Ray Mercer, but Mike Tyson will hand him his head on a platter."

Through it all, Evander Holyfield kept right on smiling. He turned a deaf ear to all of the remarks and continued to attend to business—working out each and every day, refining his magnificent physique, preparing himself just as thoroughly as he had prepared himself almost nine years earlier when I'd first seen him battle Carlos DeLeon.

Of course, you already know the rest of the story. Thirty-one months after losing the title to Michael Moorer, Evander calmly stepped through the ropes in Vegas and promptly beat the living hell out of Mike Tyson to regain that which Holyfield has always vowed was rightfully his, the heavyweight championship of the world.

While Holyfield surpassed all obstacles by turning it up a notch and working even harder, Riddick Bowe was confronting less obtrusive difficulties and doing what he has always done best, ducking responsibility and skulking away. The man with the superior tools, the greater gifts, continued to quit on himself.

People believe that everything changes as time marches on. But the truth is, the *real* things never change. Those possessing courage persist. Those who lack it merely exist.

Eddie Futch, whom I always call Mr. Futch, is one of the greatest trainers of all time. Besides being brilliant, he is a gentleman possessing an extraordinary good nature and unremitting patience. But even Mr. Futch has his limits. Not too long ago, he pulled Riddick Bowe aside and said, "I cannot deal with this anymore. I can't deal with someone who has the tools that you have, yet continues to abuse them. You say you'll stay in shape, but you don't. You say you'll train, but you don't. Of all the fighters I have been around in this business, you could be as good as any. But you won't listen to me. You think you have all the answers, but you don't. I've had it. I'm done with you. I'm gone."

And once Mr. Futch walked away from Bowe, there was nothing to stop Bowe from walking away from himself.

The real tragedy of Riddick Bowe and people like him is that, although possessing all the physical attributes—strength and size, a good chin, and a pretty good ticker from bell to bell—these wondrous gifts are of little value unless counterbalanced with discipline. Bowe had little self-control. His best weight was 224, but it was nothing for him to balloon to 280. He wouldn't tend to business. He wouldn't pay the price. He sidestepped through life, always looking for the easy way out.

If Riddick Bowe would have disciplined himself and done everything that had to be done, all the time, he would still be the heavyweight champion of the world today and long into the foreseeable future. That this never happened is a shame, yet Bowe has only himself to blame. He had all the answers, and he thought people like Mr. Futch were idiots. Bowe continued to quit. Bad habits never die.

Like so much of today's society, Riddick Bowe sought easy answers to difficult questions. He was always looking for the quick fix instead of employing the tried-and-true remedy of hard work and perseverance. Early in 1997, however, given his penchant for laziness, he perplexed me even further by enlisting in the Marine Corps.

"It's been a lifetime dream," Bowe said the day he arrived for boot camp at Parris Island, South Carolina.

Of course, I wished him well, hoping this would be his big chance to take control of his life. I figured once he got into boot camp, got his ears back, and did everything that he had to do, he would find out what life was all about. The Marines would surely enhance his character and his ability to realize his full potential.

I should have known better. When Bowe arrived at PI, he bumped headfirst into reality. It was the shock of a lifetime, because he couldn't sleep late into the morning and he couldn't eat what he wanted to eat. Drill instructors told him what to do and when to do it. Worse yet, they *demanded* that he show some personal discipline.

It proved to be too much to ask of Riddick Bowe, and he quit after only nine days in the Corps.

"He had trouble adapting," said Marine Major Rick Long, a Parris Island spokesman. "The bottom line is if you don't want to be a Marine, you won't be one."

Or a successful prizefighter for any length of time either.

No matter who you are or what magnificent tools you might have, quitting is a cancerous habit that eats away at your self-respect. Life's losers absolve themselves of responsibility. But those who hang tough, those who knuckle down and say "The hell with it, I'm gonna survive no matter what," these are the men and women who eventually make it to the top. And stay there.

Evander Holyfield has maximized his better-than-average tools. Superimpose his will, his heart, his desire, his attending to business and doing the right thing on top of his God-given talents, and you have a true champion. Not just a heavyweight champion in the prizefighting ring, but a heavyweight champion of life.

Just remember this: You weren't put here to take up space. Make things happen, dammit. Just do it. Get the job done. Don't cheat yourself. Let the other guy be the whimpering fool, while you kick butt and take names.

God help us, but if the world ever again goes to war, I want Evander Holyfield in that foxhole with me, because I know I will survive and be able to return home to my beautiful wife and darling sons.

But if I am to be guarded by underachievers, then I figure I'm in trouble.

A Working Man's Working Man

If I had to pick one principle that best characterizes my philosophy, it would be this: There is right, there is wrong, and each of us has choices. The choice we pick determines our future.

Although I believe that the choice between good and evil is life's most crucial moral dilemma, I am not so naïve as to presume I have all of the answers. I have spent a lifetime being knocked on my butt and struggling back onto my feet. I know I've said this a million times before, but all that matters is that I chose not to stay down.

Admittedly, there is a perverse irony about the choices I have made. On one hand, I am a district court judge, a sworn officer of the law. Yet my hobby is refereeing prizefights, a profession replete with young fighters making an honest living doing what some of them once did for kicks on the streets. As a vocation, boxing is the French Foreign Legion of inner-city delinquents, and its grand arena, more often than not, is a gambling casino.

In court, my job is the administration of justice in accordance with the applicable law. In the ring, my job is to serve as a buffer between violent conflict and injury, my primary focus being the fighters' adherence to protocol, the principal ensurer of pugilistic justice.

In both instances I am an arbiter, a mediator between right and wrong. While my devotion to boxing is almost as strong as my dedication to the legal process, the gulf separating these different worlds is not as wide as you might imagine. I have seen as much contempt for law and order in the courtroom as I have seen disdain for common decency by boxing's flesh merchants, the scheming managers and promoters whose only goal is to make money.

Although neither domain is perfect, there exists within each a strong thread of ethics fashioned from the truisms that money can't buy you respect, and that there are indeed consequences for your actions. As long as this continues to flourish, at least as the ideal, I will continue to walk both paths with a clear conscience.

It is no secret that I loathe all that is incorrigible. But it would be foolish of me to stipulate that the living of my life has been void of errors of commission or omission. I have made as many mistakes in the ring as I have outside its constricting arena. In the course of this roller-coaster journey, however, my education was furthered. I discovered that you cannot have honor without virtue; that in order to have justice, you sometimes must embrace injustice; and that the moral fiber of an individual is not determined by the cut of his or her clothes. As such, sworn officers of the court—be they lawyers or law enforcement officials—are not immune to criminal behavior.

While, at times, it has been one hell of an educational process, I have come to realize that nothing irritates me more than when someone violates trust, either yours or mine. I was raised in an age when commitments were bound by the strength of your word and your handshake, and the violation of these commitments was unthinkable. It was a time when corruption and vice were the outgrowth of only the lowest class of individual.

Today, however, no segment of society is spared this shame. And the saddest commentary of all is that we can no longer afford to have blind faith in those entrusted with the greatest of powers— politicians, doctors, lawyers, bankers, and police officers. To do so is to encourage disaster, for there is no way of knowing if these individuals are as crooked as the bastards dominating the headlines of yesterday's newspapers.

Such has become the corruption of life's toughest decision, the choice between right and wrong.

∽∽∽∽∽∽

I have not been immune to personal setbacks. At the same time, I have no one to blame but myself for most of these disasters. I have had choices to make and damned if I didn't make the wrong ones from time to time. In that regard, the defining moment in my life was my failure to make the 1960 Olympic boxing team. No matter where I am today or what I'm doing, I'll find myself thinking, "If only I had . . ." I'm sure you know the refrain as well as I do: *If only I had not been such an idiot.*

While the best recourse is to move forward and do your best not to repeat those mistakes, sometimes it's impossible to outrun yesterday. It's relatively easy to redeem yourself when you're fortunate enough to have a second and third chance. But when you have one and only one shot at doing something right, and you subsequently blow it out of your own stupidity, then the sting of defeat lingers forever.

My failure was the direct result of my refusal to listen to my boxing coach coupled with my overconfidence. I thought I was the only person at the Olympic Trials who knew of Kenny Lane, the Muskegon, Michigan, super lightweight–junior welterweight champion, one of the greatest left-handed fighters of all time.

The Olympic Trials were held in the Cow Palace in San Francisco, and my first fight was against the U.S. Navy champion, Victor Lopez of Price, Utah. Although Lopez was a pretty good fighter, I managed to defeat him and then took a seat in the grandstands to watch Phil Baldwin, the southpaw who would be my opponent in the semifinals.

As I've said before, my style in the ring was no big secret. I'd jump all over you, never backing up an inch. Before the biggest fight of my life, however, I came down with a bad case of stupidity and decided to box Baldwin—I thought I could outpoint him. After all, Joe Bliss, my good friend and University of Nevada-Reno teammate, was a southpaw and we must have sparred against each other for at least five hundred rounds, so I figured I knew every trick a left-hander could pull.

"I'm going to outbox this guy," I told Jimmie Olivas, my coach. "Baldwin won't know what to do because he's never faced a good southpaw before."

I thought Olivas was going to have a heart attack. "For Christ's sake, Mills, forget that boxing shit. Fight your fight. Just jump on him and kick his ass."

But I figured I knew what was best. I would come out boxing and Baldwin wouldn't have a clue. I'd nail him with my jab, and then finish him off. It was going to be a piece of cake. In my mind, at least.

The reality of the fight was that no matter what I did, Baldwin did it three times better. He won the first round easily and I fared no better in the second. I finally smartened up in the final round and reverted to my original style. Although I managed to win that third round, Baldwin got his hand raised and subsequently went on to represent the United States at the Rome Olympics while I got to make the long, sobering drive back home to Reno in the company of my own stupidity.

Before I did so, though, I cornered Baldwin after the fight and asked, "How the hell did you know ahead of time what I was going to do? You made it look so easy."

Baldwin grinned at me and said, "You don't know where I'm from, do you. I'm from Muskegon and I learned everything I know from Kenny Lane."

I felt like an idiot, and justifiably so. If I had only listened to sound reasoning, maybe I could have beaten Phil Baldwin and made the trip to Rome and squared off against Italy's Nino Benvenuti, the eventual gold medal winner. Had that happened, I would not have had to endure the verbal butt kicking from Jimmie Olivas on the drive home. He just wouldn't let up, hammering on me and hammering on me.

Finally, just as we got to Auburn, California, I said, "Look, Jimmie, I know I didn't fight a good fight, and I know I've got this coming. But I've been chewed and chewed as long as I want to get chewed. If you want me to get out of the car and hitchhike back, I'll do it. But I don't want you to talk to me anymore."

To this very day, whenever I face a tough decision, whether it is in the courtroom, at home, or in the prizefight ring, I will close my eyes and think back to that gut-wrenching drive home from the Olympic Trials. And that's when Jimmie Olivas's voice comes back to me, as haunting and condemning as ever: "Dammit, Mills, if you would only have listened . . ."

That Olympic trials failure was over. I had my big chance, and I didn't make the most of it. But I refused to let that failure destroy me. I kept battling away at other goals, successfully becoming a prizefighter, a trial prosecutor for the district attorney's office and a boxing referee, a district attorney and then a district judge.

And in court, when a defendant ducks responsibility by saying his or her troubles are the result of drug addiction, abusive parents, or crap like that, I think back to my fight against Phil Baldwin at the Olympic Trials and shake my head in dismay. That's why I tell the defendant, "No, your problems are not because your daddy yelled at you. It's not because you weren't breast-fed or because your mama didn't change your diapers. The problem is *you!* And until you get it together, these problems will follow you."

From the moment of my failure at San Francisco's Cow Palace, I began working on myself. I began listening to the voice of experience and heeding the dictates of my heart instead of my head. I turned everything around by following that very narrow path on the side of law and order, and concentrated on how my behavior affected others. I followed the good examples set by others and tried to set a good example myself.

And while I proved to be very human, making more mistakes that I care to admit, I kept swinging away and eventually attained my dreams. More important, I have done so with a clear conscience.

∞∞∞∞∞

Because of my strong conviction that we are always fighting the battle between right and wrong and must continue to stay on the side of what is right and good, obtaining a law degree and working for the Washoe County District Attorney's Office as a trial prosecutor in 1972 was a natural progression. I became one of the "King's Men," an advocate for the people, a staunch upholder of law and order. And in the course of doing my duty, I convicted twenty-two murderers in sixteen separate cases. While that might sound impressive, I'm also a firm believer that if you show me a prosecutor who brags about his or her conviction rate, I'll show you a prosecutor who hasn't tried enough cases.

Of course, my tenacity didn't endear me to public defenders. I remember Shelly O'Neill, a public defender in the late 1980s, relating a story about me to William Nack of *Sports Illustrated*. She said that she approached me one day about an indigent client she was representing and that I said, "All you defense lawyers are alike. I

wouldn't piss on you if you were on fire." As I recall the conversation, I didn't say *all* defense lawyers. I said *some.*

When I ran against Shelly for district judge in November 1990, another defense lawyer said that his worst nightmare would be having to say "Good morning, Judge Lane." Such comments are a compliment, even when courtroom antagonists referred to me as a pit bull. I want to stay in the pit. You show me a good loser, and I'll show you someone I want to fight every day. The bottom line is I might not get a high score on an IQ test, but I'll sure as hell try to outwork you. That's the name of the game.

I've always been a demanding, nonsensical workaholic, an individual whose demeanor is best summarized by the late Harry S Truman. "I don't give 'em hell," the president once said. "I just tell the truth and they think it's hell." And that's me in a nutshell. I'm picky, I'm punctual, and I'm particular in my likes and dislikes. I have a hard-line political stance, meaning I'll go with the best man or woman for the job, regardless of party affiliation. I vehemently support the rights of our law-abiding citizens to bear arms. I believe in the death penalty, meaning it's cheaper to water a poppy than feed people like Sirhan Sirhan, Charles Manson, Susan Smith, or Jeffrey Dahmer. And I think affirmative action is asinine. If you ask my opinion, be prepared for the truth as I interpret it. And if you don't like what I have to say, I'm not going to lose any sleep over it.

My bottom line is that despite being born to an affluent family, I am at heart and in principle a blue-collar guy. I work for the citizens of Washoe County, state of Nevada. My loyalty is to all of the citizens, not just the rich and the powerful. I'm a working man's working man. I'm a man of faith and conscience who has an immeasurable amount of love for family, friends, and country. I also have set rigid standards for myself and I expect others to do likewise. And if they don't give a damn about self-control and self-respect, I don't want anything to do with them.

For example, despite being chief criminal deputy, I ended up leaving the DA's office in 1979 because I lost confidence in my boss, then–district attorney Cal Dunlap. Working with Dunlap was hell on earth. He was one of those people who believed in micro-managing. Not content to trust his underlings to do their jobs, he just had to have his hand in everything. It got so bad that I couldn't make a decision without Dunlap's approval, and, in essence, I ended up being nothing more than a high-paid trial deputy. I wasn't a supervisor of anything, not even myself.

The ultimate insult to my integrity occurred midway through the first year of Dunlap's term, when he was out of the state conducting some bullshit investigation. It was very important that I speak with him, because I needed his opinion concerning a case I was working on. But when I explained to Judy Zupan, Dunlap's secretary, the urgency of the situation, she said that she was under strict orders not to divulge Dunlap's whereabouts.

"Dammit, Judy, I'm his chief assistant and I need to speak to the boss," I said.

"I realize that, and I feel real bad about this," Judy said. "But all I can tell you is that he's in Louisiana doing a special investigation."

"Okay," I said, "but you tell him that when he drives his Yankee ass back in here, I've got something to say to him."

There comes a time in everyone's life when you know, without a doubt, that you have made the right choice, the right decision. When Dunlap returned to work, I went into his office and closed the door. Without preamble, I said, "Listen, I don't care about what you do in your private life. But you are not immortal; you could die. And I'm your chief deputy of this county. If you trust me, you tell me everything so I can do what has to be done. But if you don't trust me, then fire me."

Dunlap apologized and said he would not make that mistake again, but I told him it was too late. And that's when he really insulted me by saying, "Mills, we have a lot of cases going on and I really need your help. If you stay with me, you can have this job when I leave."

To which I responded, "Just who in the hell do you think you are? The people of this county will make that decision, not you." With that, I turned on my heel and walked away from a bureaucratic nightmare.

I ended up working for Sheriff Bob Galli as a chief deputy sheriff and a special prosecutor for the next two years. Galli and the men and women working with him were some of the finest people I've ever been around. I learned a lot about criminal investigation from them, which helped me greatly in November 1982 when I was elected district attorney of Washoe County. Yet despite my outspoken views of law and order, not everyone knew where I was coming from when I assumed the DA's job the following January. The bottom line is I firmly believe that our courts have gone too far in protecting the rights of criminals. While this is sometimes not a popular opinion outside of the law enforcement community, it is a conclusion I had reached through hands-on experience.

For instance, early in my first term as DA, I was called to the jail late one night because of a shooting incident. An elderly California gentleman and his wife had been gambling at one of the downtown casinos, and shortly after they returned to their RV at the downtown RV Park, a hoodlum broke into their trailer. The old man, who must have been about eighty, grabbed his .22 revolver and shot the thief in the leg. When I was summoned to the police station, the elderly couple was in the interrogation room, scared to death, worrying if the old man was going to be charged with a felony.

I was briefed by the head investigator and then went into the interrogation room to get the old guy's story, which tallied with the police version. Having no problem with what the old man had done, I opened the door and told him and his wife that they were free to go.

"You're going to let me go?" said the old man, dumbfounded.

I said, "Sure, you shot a thief in your house. That's not illegal."

"Gee, in California I'd be prosecuted for this," said the old man. And he might have been correct.

And then when I told the head cop to return the gentleman's pistol, the old man again looked at me with surprise and said, "You mean I get to keep my gun?"

"Hell, yes," I told him. "You might have to shoot another one of them thieving sonsabitches before you leave town." Of course, I was hoping he wouldn't go that far, because I wanted to go back to sleep.

But think about it for a second. Here was a law-abiding citizen in his home, defending himself, his family, and his property against a hoodlum. The elderly gentleman was disadvantaged age-wise, meaning physical confrontation was out of the question. So he did what he felt was appropriate, which in my view was very appropriate, and he has to worry about his government prosecuting him?

Far too often, though, it seems as if the system has been turned upside down. That's why in 1990, when I ran for district judge, I chose a platform based on the premise that judges are too powerful. The question then and now in litigation is not "Who did it?" but "Did the police officer blunder?" And that's wrong. It's frustrating to go before an incompetent judge who doesn't know what the hell is going on and makes rulings that extend the rights of criminals more than required by the Constitution.

I don't wish to imply that the legal system is falling apart. But I do think there's room for big improvement. The genesis of injustice falls on the shoulders of judges who unnecessarily create impediments to the search for the truth.

One of the impediments that we do accept is the Fifth Amendment, which says that a prosecutor can't force a defendant to testify against himself. That is a part of English common law, the basis for our judicial system. But the exclusionary rule about holding out evidence that shows truth, even if the evidence is tainted, is not countenanced in England. For example, let's say you have a bad cop, a rogue cop who violates people's rights. When we encounter such an individual, we must put him behind bars. But our legal system takes it a step farther. Because this rogue cop violated a criminal's rights in the obtaining of vital evidence, that evidence is not allowed to be presented to the jury. Our judicial system does this in order to change police procedures. The idea is to send a strong message that *all* police officers must follow strict guidelines in the search for the truth. But what the system really ends up doing is punishing society by allowing a murderer to go free. Where's the justice in that?

Even when that officer commits an unlawful search in good faith, not realizing that he or she is doing something wrong, the evidence is thrown out. Again, the theory is to teach the police a lesson. But if they didn't know they were doing wrong, it doesn't teach anybody anything. Instead, you've allowed a murderer or a rapist to go free to murder or rape again, and the whole concept of justice is flawed.

Some of our court decisions are downright ridiculous. A great example of this is *Morris v. Slappy,* in which the Ninth Circuit Court of Appeals reversed a conviction in California because it felt that the defendant did not have a meaningful relationship with his attorney, whatever the hell that's supposed to mean. You've got a right to competent counsel and a fair trial, but the quality of your relationship with your lawyer isn't addressed in the Constitution. When the Ninth Circuit made that asinine ruling, it did not advance the search for the truth. Thank God far more enlightened minds prevailed and the Ninth Circuit decision was reversed by the Supreme Court, allowing the conviction to stand.

Another impediment in the search for truth occurs, for example, when you have a defendant who does not talk to the police, but then takes the witness stand and gives his or her version of what occurred. The natural inclination would be for the prosecution to say in cross-examination, "Wait a minute. Two years after the murder you're telling us what occurred. Why didn't you tell us that two years ago?" Of course, I don't think there's anything wrong in asking the defendant that question. But in *Doyle v. California,* the Supreme Court said you couldn't do this because it's commenting on the defendant's right to remain silent. Again, that's bullshit.

Another thing that needs to be corrected in our judicial system is there's just too much red tape involved in the process. The death penalty is the greatest example of this. Either we have the death penalty or we don't. Now I don't believe in executing someone if there is the slightest question as to his or her guilt. If so, delay the execution of sentence indefinitely. But when you have an instance where guilt has been determined without a shadow of doubt, yet execution is delayed by a glut of innocuous appeals, the appellate process becomes a fraud.

Take, for example, Ricky Sechcrest, whom I successfully prosecuted for sexually abusing and murdering two little girls. He has been on Death Row since 1973. Every day that he breathes is a crying shame. His guilt has never been an issue in the appeals process. Yet there he sits, being fed and housed at the taxpayer's expense, and we can't get the job done. In that sense, there's no justice at all.

One of the arguments being used on behalf of doing away with the death penalty is that it costs more to execute the condemned than it does to keep him or her in prison for life. This is true, but the bulk of this cost is due to the proliferation of nonsensical appeals and subsequent delays in carrying out the execution. For this you can blame the judges.

The system must operate better, it must be changed. And that's one of the reasons I became a judge. I wanted to make a difference. I wanted to put aside the BS and cut to the chase. Of course, in the process of doing this, I've taken some knocks. Just as I've had convictions reversed as a prosecutor, I've had some rulings overturned on the bench. But that hasn't stopped me from saying what I think. A public official owes that to the people he works for. They should know where he stands.

So, if you want to say that my actions as a district attorney were like those of "Wyatt Earp, cleaning up the Old Wild West town," as one lawyer did a number of years back, or if my actions on the bench are like "Roy Bean, the ol' hang 'em high judge of the Wild West," as one reporter recently referred to me, then fine. In defense of that rhetoric I believe I became known as "Maximum Mills" throughout northern Nevada *only* because I don't believe in half measures, which produce half-assed results. By God, there's right and there's wrong, and everyone has choices. As such, when someone walks into the people's courtroom in which I preside and is subsequently found guilty of a crime against mankind, then if it's deserved, that person is going to feel the force of the law.

That's what the system is supposed to be all about. The jury determines guilt or innocence, and punishment is handed down based upon what's deserved. The system is not about making exceptions or a fuzzy-headed delay.

For instance, from Day One on the bench, I set the tone for punctuality. If a lawyer was late, I threatened him with a $25 fine. There was one warning. If he or she did not heed the message, they had to dig into their wallet. The money was used to purchase books for our law library, which was increased substantially my first year as a judge.

Few books were added after that.

∞∞∞∞∞

Right or wrong, good or evil—the choice is yours. I believe that the segregation of one from the other depends on your sense of decency. It's a choice that also speaks volumes about your moral upbringing. But if you embrace the wrong choice, then it's up to others to determine your fate, and you'd better be willing to pay the price.

If I had to pick one instance that best validates my choice of law and order, and at the same time shows how I operate in the courtroom, it would be a case I handled as a special prosecutor for Sheriff Bob Galli.

In April 1981 in Yerington, Nevada, I prosecuted Red Kingsley, the sheriff of Lyon County, for lying to a grand jury. A year or so earlier, Kingsley had convinced the county commission that he needed to hire a special agent to help him track down dope dealers and other big-time criminals operating in his area. Once this action was approved, Kingsley and his special agent then conspired to have Billy Akers, a twenty-two-year-old, marginally retarded doper, rob a bank. Of course, Kingsley and his agent would capture Akers and become heroes.

And that's the way it went down. These two law enforcement officers filled Billy with dope and booze, and then waited a few blocks away from the bank in order to "capture" Akers after he had made the big heist. The townspeople bought the self-serving charade lock, stock, and barrel.

Akers was tried and convicted, despite the fact that the robbery was really Sheriff Kingsley's idea. Billy Akers was locked up and the matter was quickly forgotten. But later on, when some governmental problems cropped up and a grand jury convened to look into the matter, Sheriff Kingsley was put on the witness stand. By this time, the good people of Lyon County had begun to doubt the sheriff's veracity. Therefore, the first question they asked of him was, "Did you know of that bank robbery before it occurred?"

When Kingsley said he did not, he was indicted for perjury. In short order, the district attorney bowed out of the case and I was brought in.

Howard McKibben, who is now an outstanding federal judge, was the presiding judge in this affair and he settled in to listen to Sheriff Kingsley's version of the truth as opposed to the prosecution's. Once we rested our case, Judge McKibben was every bit as stunned as I was when one of the defense's first witnesses got on the stand and shot himself in the foot. The guy was a former county commissioner and obviously the defense council had not prepared him properly.

"Can you please tell us what Mr. Kingsley told you . . ." the defense council started to say, but I interrupted him and objected, telling Judge McKibben that this was hearsay.

McKibben said, "Well, Mr. Lane, I believe you may be right, but I'm gonna let it in."

The defense council smiled at me in triumph and then turned once again to the county commissioner and asked, "Did you talk to Mr. Kingsley before the robbery?"

"Yes sir," said the commissioner. Of course, I was waiting for the guy to say that Kingsley didn't know anything about the robbery. Instead, the commissioner said, "Yes, I talked to the sheriff at eight-thirty that morning at Mound House," which is a town about thirty miles away from Yerington, "and the sheriff said 'I've got to get back as quickly as I can, because it's going down at nine o'clock.' "

After the next recess, the defense council made a motion to recall the commissioner. The commissioner got back on the stand and changed his story. He told the judge and jury that he had not meant to say what he'd said earlier, that he was confused and had it wrong. What a fraud!

Every day that defense counsel would drive into Lyon County in a Porsche and wearing his fancy suit; people just couldn't help but notice this high-powered city boy descending upon them. On the other hand, I lived in Lyon County during the entire trial, and everyday I arrived at court wearing my JC Penney's suit coat, which was a little frayed at the cuffs. My shirts didn't fit exactly right either.

And whereas that high-powered city lawyer spoke to the jury with highfalutin words they couldn't understand, when my time came to refute the altered testimony given by the former county commissioner, I shuffled up to the witness chair and sat down, then turned toward the jury and gave them my best down-home country smile.

"Ladies and gentlemen, you're not gonna hear any big words from me because I don't know any," I said. "Why, I'm just a country boy; I'm rural. In fact, I'm out here in Yerington, Nevada, and when I smell alfalfa and cowshit, I love it. It smells good."

What I was thinking, but didn't dare say to the jury, was, "You and me are of the same vein. We love the smell of alfalfa and cowshit, and we can sure as hell recognize the odor of bullshit when we smell it."

What I said was, "Yes, ladies and gentlemen, you live in a beautiful part of the county. In fact, this has got to be the prettiest valley in Nevada. But you do have some terrible problems here. Your sheriff crawled up to this witness stand and took an oath to God, which he promptly violated. Now that's bad enough. But then one of your county fathers crawled up here and took an oath to God, then lied to you and me and the judge and to everybody else in Lyon County. What you need to do is take his testimony and put it in a garbage bag and carry it to the dump and bury it deep, because that is exactly where it belongs."

As I like to say, Red Kingsley was tried before an unbiased and unprejudiced jury. And he is no longer the sheriff of Lyon County. Justice prevailed.

Sanctioned Deception

One of the greatest upsets in sports history didn't really happen.

To hear Don King and his sidekick Jose Sulaiman tell it, the devastating flurry of punches by Buster Douglas that battered Mike Tyson were an illusion. The right uppercut that lifted Tyson off the mat, the crushing left and right hands that snapped his head back and forth, and the left hook that finally chopped Tyson into delirium were merely figments of our imagination.

"No, no, no. Buster Douglas was knocked out. The referee did not do his job. Those are the facts," King was screaming moments after Tyson rolled over on his stomach midway through the tenth round, located his mouthpiece, inserted it backwards into his mouth, then struggled to his feet and collapsed into the arms of Octavio Meyran Sanchez, the referee in question.

Sulaiman, the *generalissimo* of the World Boxing Council, looked at King and nodded his head in agreement, then turned to an associate and said, "But I am very confused."

Many of us shared that same opinion, because on the night of February 11, 1990, in the Tokyo Dome, King and Sulaiman—in a desperate bid to save not only Tyson's butt and his WBC heavy-weight crown, but their multimillion-dollar meal ticket as well—attempted one of the boldest heists in prizefighting's shady history. The plan called for the referee to be the fall guy. But when Octavio Meyran Sanchez refused to play along with the con job, everything fell apart.

The controversy began in the eighth round when, with little time remaining, Tyson floored Douglas with a right uppercut. When Douglas's butt hit the mat, the timekeeper began his count. Instead of picking up the cadence from the timekeeper, Meyran allegedly began his own count two seconds later. Of course, Don King's memory is so selective that he expected everyone at ringside to forget the following:

- That although Douglas was down, he was far from being out. He was alert. So alert, in fact, that he slammed his left fist on the canvas because he was upset with himself for having been careless.

- That Douglas had his eyes riveted on Meyran, watching the referee's hands as the count progressed from three to six. And when the count reached nine, Douglas was already on his feet and clearheaded.

- That up until the moment Tyson landed that punch—his *only* solid shot of the entire fight—he had been getting the hell beat out of him. Douglas turned Tyson's legs to jelly in the fifth round with a devastating right, and in the next round Tyson's left eye started to swell shut. Douglas closed it completely in the ninth with a four-punch flurry that sent Tyson flying into the ropes.

None of this meant diddly-squat, however, because Don King said it didn't. "The first knockout obliterated the second knockout," King shouted moments after the fight.

Meyran, however, defended his performance by saying, "I gave Douglas a count of nine."

King, furious that Meyran refused to play the game, stormed off in search of other vigilantes. In short order, he rounded up Sulaiman and WBA president Gilberto Mendoza and a few members of the Japan Boxing Commission, and then huddled with them behind locked doors in the Tokyo Dome.

Two hours later, King emerged and told the media, "I have lodged an official protest," to which the media inquired, "How could or why would a promoter of an event lodge a protest on one particular fighter's behalf?"

As expected, King went nuts, screeching, "I am the promoter for both fighters. All I want is for fair play to prevail. Fair play. That's all we're looking for. No emotionalism, no sensationalism— just the facts. That's why we have commissioners. You do your thing and I'll do my thing. I may not have the clout to do this. But there's been a grave injustice here."

With that, King and his minions huddled for another three hours behind closed doors. And when Sulaiman and Mendoza finally emerged, the media swore that although they saw the lips of both commissioners moving, they were certain it was Don King's voice they heard declare, "The official result of the fight will be decided by the WBC and WBA within two weeks." The IBF immediately recognized Douglas as the champion and stood its ground.

The members of the media looked at one another in disbelief as Sulaiman sputtered, "We now have two results: Buster Douglas winning and Mike Tyson winning. At the moment, I am suspending the recognition of anybody as champion."

"Why are you doing this?" one of the reporters asked. To which Sulaiman responded, "Boxing is a sport with rules and regulations. If we do not stand for rules and regulations, what do we stand for?"

Damn good question. The crux of King's folly was that Meyran had given Douglas fourteen seconds to get to his feet instead of ten, which is a totally asinine argument. As a practical matter, there is not a boxing referee in the world who actually gives you ten seconds. What you get is a *count* of ten. Put a stopwatch to it, and that count may actually be eleven or twelve seconds or it might even be only nine seconds. But it is rarely ten on the nose, and everyone in the business knows that.

All King and Sulaiman were really worried about was preserving Tyson's hold on the title. He was their meal ticket, the flesh that paid for the villas and vichyssoise, the Porsche and the Mercedes, and the $800 suits. By God, something had to be done. So it was in those hours after the fact that King and Sulaiman played the role of revisionists and declared that, after careful consideration, tapes of the bout clearly showed the errors of Meyran's ways.

"Buster Douglas was knocked out," said King, explaining why the heavyweight title should still belong to Tyson. "The referee did not do his job and panicked."

Meyran, however, continued to stand his ground. Refusing to be intimidated, as are some shameless referees, Meyran again said, "No, I gave Douglas a count of nine."

Of course, the charade ended almost as quickly as it was concocted. Once King returned to New York City, he was so vilified in the newspapers and on television that he quickly changed his tune. Buster Douglas was indeed the new champ and almost everyone would live happily ever after.

∞∞∞∞∞∞

Discounting prizefighting's fragile integrity, the biggest casualty of the Tokyo farce was referee Octavio Meyran Sanchez. He stood tall and refused to back down, despite King's rhetoric and threats.

Here was something unique, a man standing his ground calling things as he saw them. His honesty and self-respect were apparently more important to him than anything else, and for this he should have been universally praised. Instead, it is the contention of several boxing insiders that Meyran was blacklisted. There is, of course, no proof to substantiate such an allegation. But then again, as far as I know, Meyran has not refereed a WBC title fight since that fateful night.

Professional boxing needs men like Meyran. The irony of the situation, though, is that individuals such as Meyran need boxing. Because refereeing fees are a substantial part of their incomes, they are in a very vulnerable position. As such, a handful of highly suspect entrepreneurs can twist the financial screws to such an extent that normally righteous individuals might discard their honesty and go along with someone else's dubious program.

I'm immune to that crap, because I have "fuck you" money. My father was an industrious man with a strong eye on the future and he created a trust on my behalf, which I inherited on my twenty-first birthday. It was a start, and if I worked and saved it would put me in good financial shape.

The best thing you can pass on to your children is opportunity. But if you can pass on both opportunity and security, they will have the world by the tail. When you embark on life with such an edge, the percentages are in your favor. If you try your hand at a certain profession only to discover you don't care for it, you can reach for another brass ring without fear of drowning in a sea of debt. Because you have a monetary cushion, you need not be held hostage by a job you despise. In essence, my father gave me the greatest gift of all: the opportunity to fail on my own terms.

Or as Mickey Duff, the British boxing manager, once put it, "Know why I like having you as the referee, Mills? It's because I know the fight will be on the up and up. My man will get a fair shot, because you'll damn well make sure he does. And you'll do this because you have 'fuck you' money. You have a regular day job, and while it's nice to get assigned a certain fight, you don't have to be assigned. That's why no one can intimidate you, or buy you or sell you, which is rare in this business."

Mickey's compliment is right on the money, because I'm *not* for sale. My principles and my integrity do not have a price tag. The bottom line is that I have no fear of artificial power or counterfeit threats. And if you attempt to sell me ill-gotten goods or endeavor to muscle me in any form or fashion, my response is simple: "Fuck you!"

As such, prizefighting's dubious characters have always given me a wide berth. I guess they respect a man of few words.

∞∞∞∞∞

Don King reminds me a lot of Rasputin, the Siberian monk who attached himself like a leech to the Russian czar Nicholas II and his wife. As the story goes, despite numerous attempts on Rasputin's life, including feeding him enough poison to kill any ten men, the court sorcerer just couldn't be knocked down for the count.

And so it is with King, who has had the hounds of hell on his heels for more than a decade. The IRS went after him in the mid-eighties, charging him with evading taxes in excess of $1 million, and King beat the rap. Most recently King is facing nine counts of wire fraud from the federal government. He has also bumped heads with the FBI, numerous grand juries, and, to hear him tell it, the mob and Interpol. Regardless of the odds stacked against him, King somehow managed to dodge the silver bullet.

Or as Bill Cayton, Mike Tyson's former manager, once said, "Don King can cast a spell over people that makes Svengali look like a rank amateur."

This may be true, but my thoughts concerning the kingpin of prizefighting are rather harmless. I can tell you that, despite the rapid advance of old age, King remains a promoter extraordinaire. He also continues to be a damned smart businessman, although that is somewhat questionable in light of his guilt-by-association in the Oliver McCall and Henry Akinwande disasters.

Regardless of King's pathetic performance of late, the bottom line is people can't make money in prizefighting unless they have a brilliant business sense. And in the past forty years, I have seen no one do this any better than Don King.

In the early 1980s, I was assigned to referee a middleweight bout at Caesars Palace in Las Vegas between Dwight Davidson and Curtis Parker. The fight created a little excitement because everyone had great hopes for Parker, a very compact fighter. Davidson, a big, tall, rangy guy, was the unknown factor. He hadn't been much of a fighter in the amateurs and his only claim to fame, other than being in Don King's stable, was that he had been a college wrestler at the University of Toledo.

The day of the fight I went to King's suite to get my meal tickets and ended up sitting down and chatting with Jim Deskin, who at that time was the executive director of the Nevada State Athletic Commission. Next thing we knew, King burst into the room clad in only his underwear, with one of his business associates hot on his heels.

"Davidson wants another $5,000 on top of what he's getting?" King said, incredulously.

"Yeah, five grand. But we don't have to do it, we've already got a contract," the business associate said to King. "If he doesn't play ball, it's breach of contract and we can get him banned. Is that what you want me to tell him?"

King closed his eyes for a second, then said, "No, I'm gonna give him the extra $5,000."

"You don't have to do that," replied the business associate.

"I know," said King, "but this kid might fight for the title one day, and I want him in my stable."

Without consulting either his lawyers or accountants, Don King made a sound business decision in the time it takes to bat an eye. That says all you need to know about the man's business sense.

Of course, I also believe that people should be paid what they're entitled, and that they shouldn't be stripped and left penniless once their usefulness in the ring is finished. Whether or not King falls into this category is beyond me. I have heard the allegations made against him by some of his fighters, most notably former heavy-weight champion Tim Witherspoon and superlightweight Julio Cesar Chavez. But all I know is what I read. Therefore, I am not, at this time, prepared to make a judgment.

My thoughts regarding Don King are limited to cold, hard facts. I know that he was a numbers runner in Cleveland and, according to police reports, in 1954 he shot and killed a thief who tried to rob his betting parlor. The district attorney, however, declined to prosecute, calling the shooting justifiable homicide. In 1966, King was arraigned on a second-degree murder charge for beating to death Sam Garrett, one of his numbers runners in Cleveland. The prosecutor and jury did its job, convicting King of murder. The judge, however, reduced the charge to manslaughter and sentenced King to serve the minimum one-to-twenty stretch in the state penitentiary.

King did not idle away his time in prison. He read everything he could get his hands on, and out of that reading came knowledge. He also took whatever educational classes were available. And when he was paroled after serving only four years, King reentered society a somewhat changed man—far more astute, intelligent, and determined he would never return to the scene of his numerous past crimes. As such, when King got into the fight game, it was no small wonder that he prospered as no promoter had ever prospered before.

And in the course of becoming a multimillionaire, Don King was honored in curious fashion. He received the Urban Justice Award, was invited to the White House in 1977 for a dinner honoring the Shah of Iran, was pardoned of past sins by the governor of Ohio in the 1980s, and most recently was inducted into the International Boxing Hall of Fame in Canastota, New York.

As the man himself is so apt to say, "Only in America."

∞∞∞∞∞

The fast shuffle has always been boxing's business as usual rather than its exception. For the most part, the kids climbing into the ring are not Rhodes scholars. They are tough street kids, some of whom have trouble counting change. And while they are wise to the ways of their hustling teenage buddies, they are no match for the serious sharks lurking beside the ring apron.

That's why people like the Duvas insist that each of their fighters have his own accountant and lawyer. It's just good business sense. If you don't use the brains you were born with and refuse legitimate help from legitimate people, thus opening yourself up

177

to the possibility of buying a left-handed screwdriver, then shame on you.

One of the biggest complaints against King is the manner in which he has controlled the boxing spotlight, which is through acute manipulation. The contracts he has with fighters could be called "contracts of adhesion." If you want to fight one of his champions, King says, "Okay, but under one condition. You have to give me an option on your next two fights if your guy beats my guy."

The challenger's manager has always signed on the dotted line. There has been no *real* negotiation, there has been no *real* meeting of the minds, there has been no *real* bargaining whatsoever. Basically it's take it or leave it. As such, there is a serious legal question as to whether or not such "contracts" could stand a legal challenge in court.

Boxing is replete with hard facts, most of which have been fashioned outside the ring. The most important of these is that prize-fighting could not survive without promoters. It is people such as Don King who put on these extravaganzas, which draw fight fans and staggering amounts of pay-per-view money to the business.

While promoters are indeed the lifeblood of the discipline, that does not give them the right to bleed the poor bastards up there in the ring. But halting this practice must begin with the individual fighter. If that young man searches out a reputable manager and listens to him, putting aside his own greed and impatience in the process, he has taken the first major step. The rest is common sense. The best advice I ever received was, "If it sounds too good to be true, it ain't."

But there's one thing I can tell you about Don King: his checks don't bounce.

∞∞∞∞

Boxing is described by some in very unflattering terms, and while I don't agree with all the charges leveled at boxing, I do have to say that one of the major problems of the business is that some jurisdictions leave the naming of the officials to the discretion of the bodies sanctioning the fight. This raises some serious questions.

The alleged purpose of a sanctioning body is to add credibility to the event. If that is indeed its aim, then the most legitimate thing it could do would be to take its fingers out of everyone's pockets and relinquish its bureaucratic stranglehold on the fight's procedural machinery. If, for example, a championship fight is being staged in Las Vegas, which means it comes under the jurisdiction of the Nevada State Athletic Commission, then that commission should have the final say as to those who will referee and score the bout. As such, these officials would be held accountable to that commission.

To do otherwise is to invite the sort of public relations nightmare that occurred in San Antonio on September 10, 1993, when Julio Cesar Chavez retained his superlightweight title against Pernell Whitaker on a draw. From what I hear, most fight people thought Whitaker won.

As expected, Whitaker felt as if he had been robbed. Lou Duva, his trainer, was a bit more precise, saying, "We got fucked!"

The Duva family, of course, promoted Whitaker, while Chavez is a long-standing member of the Don King camp. The fight was promoted by King and sanctioned by the WBC. Those are the facts.

The supposition, of course, is a long-standing one: that two of the ringside scorers were assigned by the WBC.

The bottom line is that because the WBC's fingerprints were smeared all over the scoring apparatus, the verdict was suspect. All of which would be a helluva case to take before a jury, unless, of course, it were presented in this fashion:

> *Ladies and gentlemen, while I do not believe any prizefighting judge is ordered to vote for one fighter or another, I do believe there are, at times, very subtle pressures at work. Let us suppose, just for a second, that you are one of the ringside scorers. You call Costa Rica home, yet you love traveling to the United States, especially when someone else is footing the bill.*
>
> *So here you are in San Antonio, enjoying the life of leisure, and you know three things beyond a shadow of a doubt: you have been appointed to score this fight by WBC emperor Jose Sulaiman, Julio Cesar Chavez is the WBC champion, and Chavez is promoted by Don King, who, some allege, are closely connected.*
>
> ***Question:*** *How do you score a round that's very close? Are you going to score in favor of the challenger or for the guy who just happens to be controlled by the people who are responsible for your getting this assignment?*
>
> ***Answer:*** *Do you spell Julio with a J or an H? Because of the subtle pressures—you are afraid that if you don't keep the big boys happy you won't be invited back to America to make another fistful of greenbacks for thirty-six minutes of easy work—you give the round*

to Chavez. It's a no-brainer, ladies and gentlemen of the
jury. The state rests its case.

Of course, there is no way of proving that the scoring in the
Whitaker-Chavez fight went down in this fashion. But because
there was the likelihood that subtle pressure was at work, and
because you would have to be a fool to think otherwise, a reason-
able inference can be drawn.

In court, we call this circumstantial evidence. Far more powerful individuals and institutions have been toppled by less.

∞∞∞∞∞

Boxing has always left itself open to criticism, if not outright con-
demnation. Its recent blemishes aside, the business has at least 61
various recordkeeping affiliates worldwide and as many champions
in its seventeen weight divisions.

The math is staggering. At any given time there can be as many
as 1,037 respective champions. And I use that word loosely.

What is even more curious is that champions of one sanctioning body might not even be ranked in another sanctioning body.
Although good enough to be the champion of their respective sanctioning body, they are nonentities as far as the other sanctioning
bodies are concerned. Something stinks, and you need look no farther than to those calling the shots within the sanctimonious gov-
erning bodies of the various alphabet cartels.

Back in the 1940s and 1950s, James Norris ran prizefighting
with an iron fist and was as crooked as the day is long. The

Kefauver Commission finally indicted Norris and ran him out of town. After that, Matt Fleisher of *Ring* magazine became the God of Boxing. *Ring* was the only entity that ranked the fighters, and Fleisher had total control over who was ranked number one.

There were, however, obvious problems. If you had any talent at all, there was no way you were going to fight for the title unless you were connected. Some of the greatest fighters of all time were robbed of their glory and dignity because of the fight game's crooked way of doing business.

For example, Jake LaMotta had to go into the tank against Billy Fox in order to get his shot at the middleweight title. The Bull defeated Marcel Cerdan with a ten-round knockout on June 16, 1949, for the championship, but only because he had sold his soul.

Archie Moore didn't have to go to those extremes, but his frustration was every bit as taxing as LaMotta's. For years Joey Maxim refused to give Moore a shot at the light heavyweight title because Maxim knew Moore would whip him. Because prize-fighting had no absolute chain of command, the only way to get Maxim to fight Moore was if the boxing public demanded it. And that's what happened. The fight fans complained so loud and so often that Maxim had no choice but to fight Moore, who decisioned him in three consecutive title bouts, the first of which was on December 17, 1952.

Another guy who really got screwed over because of the ranking shenanigans was middleweight George Benton, who most experts call "the uncrowned middleweight champion of the world." On August 6, 1962, Benton defeated former champion Joey Giardello in a ten-round decision. Benton, the number-one contender at the time, should have gotten a shot at champion Dick

Tiger. But before that fight could be made, Giardello won his title back from Tiger and Benton was out in the cold.

Asked why he never gave Benton a shot, Giardello said, "I couldn't beat the guy, that's why."

To rectify such gross injustices, various sanctioning bodies sprang up overnight, all vowing to stamp out the game's greed and chicanery. Their main selling point was that their recognized champion must fight the number-one contender within a six-month time frame. If the champ refused, he would be stripped of the title. On the surface, this sounded legitimate. The real con game, however, was couched within the question: By what process will the number-one contender be determined?

When the WBA and WBC first came into existence, there was no problem with the ranking system. But after a while, people started complaining that Don King would call Jose Sulaiman, who runs the WBC, and tell him, "I want my guy, who now is number six, moved up to number one so he can fight for the title."

Of course, this allegation of skulduggery has never been proven in a court of law. Yet it is no secret that Sulaiman and King—having mastered the fine art of pugilistic alchemy, the conversion of a fighter's heart and soul into gold—have done quite nicely over the past three decades.

Although I have some problems with the sanctioning bodies, as a former fighter I would be remiss not to point out that the proliferation of organizations has greatly helped the individual fighters. Because television is where the money is, a championship fight, no matter the weight class, is a fairly easy sell. So, instead of just one champion making big money, now you've got three or four guys feeding off the same tit. If and when there is a unification fight, you are talking really, really big money. In that regard, the sanctioning bodies serve a viable purpose by creating a market for the guys up there sweating and bleeding in the ring. The downside is that these kids have to pay a sanctioning fee to belong to these various organizations.

Someone has always got a hand in your pocket, and referees are not immune to this. And while we are also expected to be dues-paying members in good standing, I decline such solidarity with my standard two-word refusal.

What I have told Marc Ratner, the executive director of the Nevada State Athletic Commission and a great man, is that at present I will not referee fights outside of this country. I will, however, travel anywhere within the country, but I will not pay dues to any of the sanctioning bodies. My commissioner assigns me to a certain fight, not the WBA or WBC or any of the other bodies. Under no conditions will I join any organizations. I will wear their logos if they want me to, but that's as far as I will go. The reason I stand fast on this is a matter of integrity.

For example, let's assume that I am a dues-paying member of the IBF, and there is a fight between the WBA champion and the IBF champion to unify the titles. Because I don't pay dues to the WBA, the people in the corner of that sanctioning body's champion most certainly would suspect me of favoritism. Right or wrong, that's just the nature of people. It's not a question of being crooked, it's a question of being human.

Because I don't belong to either sanctioning body, no one can accuse me of anything. I rest my case.

As to why there is such a proliferation of sanctioning bodies, the answer is obvious: There is a fistful of money to be made. To give you a hypothetical example, let's say some people lease a room in a city and form a corporation called the Galaxy Boxing Fraternity. To legitimize its existence, the GBF has a few gaudy championship belts manufactured, and then forms a top-ten contender list. Of course, although there is yet no title holder, the GBF is quick to remedy the situation because, after all, the public has always demanded the existence of a champion.

And so it is that the machinery cranks up, most of which is being done out of sight of the gullible public. Think nothing of the fact that the boys running the GBF just happen to be bosom-buddies with a promoter-manager by the fictional name of Jose Monarch, whose top two fighters just happen to be the number-one and number-two-ranked contenders and thus will be fighting for the title. No harm, no foul. (It may be necessary to have a confidante become the "manager" of the fighter on paper—but this can be done.)

Hiding behind that pretext, the GBF subsequently sells the rights to televise this fight to one of the cable companies for a good chunk of change and also sells the site-rights to a casino for another good chunk. Of this total outlay, the champion's purse is $3 million, while the loser is guaranteed $700,000.

The math isn't that difficult. Because the ensuing fight draws a big crowd of high rollers, the casino easily recoups its outlay. And because the two boxers are legitimate, they put on one helluva show, thus boosting the cable company's ratings, not to mention justifying the commercial rates. The boxers themselves can't complain, because they are enjoying a big payday.

But the happiest people of all are the promoter-manager and those creative geniuses running the GBF. Jose Monarch not only gets the standard one-third of the purse from both fighters, he also gets a hefty fee for promoting the fight. Despite the subsequent commercial outlays to the media for advertising and free food and beverages for the guys and gals in the pressroom, Mr. Monarch laughs all the way to the bank.

What's good for the fictional GBF, for example, is surely good enough for the rest of the nether world. So another cartel of conniving folk shake up the alphabet again, pull three letters out of the hat, and thus sanctify themselves at the expense of the boxing public.

Next thing you know, we have at least ten different sanctioning bodies and ten different champions in each of the respective sixteen weight divisions. Despite the confusion, no one except the boxing purist complains because everyone is making money hand over fist.

Human Relations: Sowing Good Seed

One of the biggest fights I've ever refereed was the June 11, 1982, match between heavyweight champion Larry Holmes and Gerry Cooney held at Caesars Palace in Las Vegas. The fight was so big that the Sports Pavilion, where Holmes had beaten Ken Norton to win the WBC title four years earlier, was used just to accommodate the thousands of sportswriters and broadcasters from all over the world who covered the fight.

What generated all the interest is that everyone seemed more concerned about the color of each fighter's skin than about their individual skills. Although Holmes-Cooney was officially billed as "boxer versus puncher" and "age versus youth," more than anything else it was "black versus white." Like it or not, fight fans turn out in record numbers whenever a black boxer is facing a white guy. And Caesars had to build a special outdoor arena that seated thirty-five thousand to accommodate those who wanted to be a part of this historic moment.

The build-up to Holmes-Cooney involved the usual "I'm gonna whip your butt" sentiments from both fighters. But what really disgusted me was the racial crap being tossed around, which the media played on for all it was worth. Much to his credit, Cooney didn't have much to say. When he did speak, his comments were confined to boxing. Holmes wasn't as selective. Because Cooney was billed as the "Great White Hope," Holmes went out of his way to degrade the challenger in front of reporters and television cameras by referring to Cooney as the "Great White Dope" and "Loony Cooney." Holmes kept running his mouth, and most of what he had to say was very offensive.

Prior to the fight, I went into Cooney's trailer at ringside and gave him the usual prefight instructions. The big guy was relaxed and as closemouthed as usual. When I visited Holmes, I told him the same thing I'd told Cooney: "I've heard all the crap that's been shown on TV and I've read all the crap that's been said in the newspapers. As of this moment, that junk is being thrown out the window. It's fight time and . . ."

Holmes didn't let me finish. "I'm here to defend my title," he said, "and if Cooney starts to give me any shit . . ."

I interrupted and said, "Just a minute. Cooney's not going to give you any shit. And if he does, I'll penalize him. And if you retaliate, then I'll penalize you, too. I expect a clean fight and that's the way it's going to be."

As it turned out, both men fought as they were supposed to—with their fists, not their mouths. Back then the title bouts were fifteen-rounders, and through the first twelve rounds it was an evenly matched fight. Holmes dropped Cooney early in the third or fourth round with a right to the head, but Cooney recovered quickly and punished Holmes pretty good with left hooks to the body as the fight wore on.

But Cooney faded in the thirteenth round, and Holmes connected with a series of overhand rights and left hooks that put Cooney down for good.

When I raised Larry Holmes's hand in victory, the fact that he was black didn't mean a damned thing. All that mattered was that the best *man* had won.

∞∞∞∞∞

I pick up the sports page and read a story about Tiger Woods. I'm told that he won three consecutive U.S. Amateur titles and that now he's taking the PGA by storm, having won the Masters and several other tournaments while earning more money in one season than anyone has ever done before. Although I know very little about golf, I'm impressed. Way to go, kid.

I read farther down the page and see a story about the Super Bowl, how each team has a great running game. The Denver Broncos' main threat is Terrell Davis, while the Green Bay Packers counter with Dorsey Levens. What I didn't know is that both played their college ball at the same time in Georgia—Davis at the University of Georgia and Levens at Georgia Tech. Again, I'm impressed, as all of us native-born Georgians should be.

I turn the page and see that the Kansas City Royals have signed career saves leader Lee Smith and former Atlanta Braves third baseman Terry Pendleton to minor league contracts. I remember Pendleton from the 1991 season, when he helped lead the Braves to the World Series and was the National League's most valuable player. You might as well call me a fan.

I turn the page again and see where Jackie Joyner-Kersee, the three-time Olympic gold medalist, has announced that her final track and field competition will be at the Goodwill Games. The news saddens me, because few athletes have added as much glamour and class to the sport.

That Woods, Levens, Davis, Pendleton, Smith, and Joyner-Kersee are black is incidental. That they currently are or once were among the greatest athletes of their time is all that matters to a real sports fan. Pendleton wasn't the best *black* third baseman in the National League in 1991. He was *the* best, period. The same can be said for Woods, Levens, Davis, Smith, and Joyner-Kersee. Skin color didn't figure into the accolades. Their races for fame and glory were won by the swiftest, and not one of them had to call upon Jesse Jackson to intervene on their behalf.

I'm dating myself, but among my favorite athletes are Joe Louis, Archie Moore, Muhammad Ali, Ernie Banks, Roberto Clemente, Hank Aaron, Bill Russell, Oscar Robinson, Jim Brown, and Walter Payton. But do you really think I sat in front of the tele-

vision and watched these men perform simply because I was trying to do my part in correcting the racial injustice practiced by our
forefathers? Hell, no. I watched and cheered them on for the same
reasons I watched and cheered for Ted Williams, Bobo Olson, Bob
Cousy, and Joe Namath. That the former group is black and the
latter white doesn't have a damned thing to do with my likes or
dislikes.

Just like countless millions of other fans, race seldom enters
into the equation when we're choosing our heroes, whether it is
within the athletic arena or up there on the big screen. My favorite
actors are Robert Duvall, Harrison Ford, and Clint Eastwood. But
I'll also pay good money to see Morgan Freeman. *Not* because he's
black, but because he's one hell of an actor.

In the same vein, if Colin Powell leads, I'll follow. And that's
not just the Marine in me talking.

Without knowing any of these gentlemen, except superficially
through TV or newspapers and magazines, we have come to idol-
ize them. Or, at the very least, respect them for what they have done
in their lives. And there's absolutely nothing wrong with that. It's
human nature.

Yet while we're colorblind in what could be called the superficial segments of daily life—sports and entertainment—we view
the truly important aspects with a far too prejudiced eye. Granted,
progress has been made from the days of Jim Crow laws and seg-
regated schools, but it still seems as if this progress is being mea-
sured in baby steps.

It mystifies me why so many people still gauge others by the
color of their skin instead of measuring the goodness of his or her

heart. I don't think it's asking too much to do otherwise. As my daddy always said, "You can't expect people to respect you unless you first show them proper respect. Sow good seed, son. Treat others as you would like to be treated and you'll experience a good harvest."

∞∞∞∞∞

My father served in the Navy as a gunnery officer during World War II, and when he finally returned home he worked a cattle farm outside of Savannah, Georgia. Within a year, however, he began looking for a bigger farm and purchased Combahee, an eleven-thousand-acre plantation about halfway between Savannah and Charleston, South Carolina.

I know this happened in 1946 because I can still close my eyes and see our home on 45th Street in Savannah and me sitting in front of a scratchy radio listening to the second Billy Conn–Joe Louis heavyweight championship fight that was contested on June 19. I remember that fight as being the greatest thing I had ever listened to. Louis knocked out Conn in the eighth round that night in New York City and it was my first introduction to boxing. I was bobbing and weaving from the seat of my pants, my excitement mounting with every punch thrown. I can still hear the announcer describing the fight: Conn going to Louis's body, Louis absorbing the punches and nailing Conn with that powerful right hand of his. At that moment emotions were stirred inside me that have yet to be stilled.

My father loved Combahee, which had been rebuilt after General Sherman burned it to the ground on his march to the sea during the War Between the States. My life took a dramatic change once we moved to the plantation because my father turned it into a working farm and he set the tone of the work at hand. One of the invaluable lessons I learned at the time was that he never asked anyone to do anything he would not do himself.

Unlike too many other people in positions of power today, my father didn't merely direct traffic, he led by example. He would roll up his sleeves and bale hay and cut timber alongside everyone else. I have always respected him for that. My father set the standard and his only demand was that everyone live up to it.

Yet whenever someone finds out that I grew up on a plantation, he or she immediately envisions me reclining in moneyed comfort and living the life of the idle rich—my feet propped up, my butt resting on a thick cushion, and the air filled with the aroma of mint juleps. These people obviously never knew my father.

He didn't believe in allowing anyone to just sit on his or her rear, and he made sure that I worked every bit as hard as the hired help. As such, my nostrils were filled with the fragrance of cowshit and my butt was riding the back of a horse as I herded cattle. At age nine I was riding on the back of a hay-baler using the leaves of a little gum tree branch to knock off the machinery's dirt and dust so that the knot-tying process wouldn't get fouled.

The following harvest I worked the fields driving a tractor, which was no big deal because I had been riding horses and herding cattle since I was eight. Driving a tractor was easy by comparison. The work was a bitch and it never ceased. City folk probably don't realize this, but when you live on a farm there is no such thing as taking a day off or sleeping in just because you're tired. I was always as tired as everyone else, but Daddy made sure we were not too tired to do our fair share of the fieldwork. There were cattle to herd, hay to cut and bale, and plenty of pulpwood and pine to put an ax or saw to—rain or shine, day or night, without fail.

My father was also a big believer in equality, and I was equally as exhausted as were the hired hands, most of whom were black people—big, strong men who just happened to be black. They were black people but never "niggers," as some of the people in our neck of the woods called them. To use derogatory language in reference to any man or woman, regardless of creed or color, would have been to negate all that my father stood for. Although he did not believe that equality was a birthright, my father did insist that all men and women *must* be treated equally. And there was no arguing that point with him. It was his law and we damned well kept it.

My father's stationery stated in Latin that "Nothing is better than farming. Nothing finer, nothing sweeter; nothing more worthy of a free man." While that may very well be a fact, I also know that nothing is harder work. We were up at the crack of dawn baling hay and busting our butts in the hay fields. And if the rains came there were other chores to do—too damned many things to do, in fact. While the work never ceased, my father truly thought that that lifestyle was the greatest thing in the world. In that regard we were quite different.

Still, I remember the years at Combahee as being a good life. There were no big shopping malls to hang out in and we seldom went into town to see a movie because the closest town, Walterboro, was eighteen miles away. We didn't go out on dates and there were no social or sports activities at school either. Life on that farm was pretty well regimented. We were bused to school, then returned home and worked the farm.

Because we lived in a big house on a big farm, my father employed a lot of hired help. Rebecca and Hedi cleaned the house and did the cooking in the morning, and Josephine, Lavinia, and Roxy took over in the evening. And like the fieldhands, almost all were black, but there was a good reason for it. This was a South in transition; we were only two generations removed from Reconstruction. Almost everyone we employed lived in the old slave quarters left over from the original plantation days. In fact, they were living in those quarters when my father bought the plantation. None of those men and women had an automobile, and even if they had one there was no place for them to go. Because they were black and racial animosity still existed among most of our neighbors, there was nowhere else for them to work. Everything considered, my daddy wasn't about to tell those folk to move out, so he hired them and paid them good wages.

As some of my childhood friends, as well as those I worked alongside, were black, I learned early on that there was nothing different between them and me. The field hands and I drank from the same water keg with the same dipper and we ate under the same tree. Their joy was my joy and their toil my toil, and I learned early on that only a fool judges someone by the tint of his or her skin.

Working with us in the fields were David Green, Eli, Benjamin "Blackie" Green, Jerry Penzil, William Graham, and Doley Mustapher, who was also in charge of the stables. Bob Rohler and Eddie Green helped my mother with the yard work. The only two white men my father employed were John Rentz, our mechanic, and Joe Garvin, a cowboy who ran the plantation store from which all the blacks purchased their supplies.

One of my best friends was Nelson Garvin, who lived about five miles away. He was the best outdoorsman I have ever met. Nelson was a great hunter and always carried a big Bowie knife that my mother had given him for Christmas. We spent a lot of our time together hunting rabbits with our beagle hounds.

My other best friend was Nicodemus "Dip" Green, who lived within rock-throwing distance of my house. My family lived in what everyone called the "Big House" and everyone else lived on "The Street," which was just a dirt road with two deep ruts and grass growing between them that ran for a quarter of a mile. On both sides of the dirt road were the old slave quarters—clapboard houses built up off the ground and supported at the corners by brick or stone foundations. There was no running water or electricity. Dip lived in such a house.

Because he was my good buddy, I was at Dip's house all the time playing and eating the bread his mamma made on her old wood-burning stove. The inside walls of his home were covered with newspapers to seal the cracks and to keep out the cold. There was no inside plumbing and each family on The Street had its own outhouse. But no one made a big deal of it, because that was the old South and such things were never given much consideration.

Of course, therein lies the anomaly of those times. There were places in Walterboro that had whites-only water fountains and blacks-only water fountains. The same with the bathrooms. But I never gave much thought to the separation of the races. When Nelson Garvin, Dip Green, and I went swimming at the pond down in the rice field we would strip naked, jump into the water, and have a good old time. It was white penises and black penises, which didn't matter because we were buddies.

Then again, that's how I was raised. I merely followed my father's example. If, when we were out in the fields, Blackie needed a drink of water, he went to the common barrel and took hold of the dipper and drank. Granted, some of the white guys who helped us in those hay fields refused to share that water and brought their own bottles. But I used the same water keg that Blackie and David Green, Eli and Jerry Penzil did.

After all, if it was good enough for my daddy it was good enough for me.

∞∞∞∞∞

Probably the most enduring lesson I learned from my father was that if you want people to treat you with respect, you first must treat them with respect. Having been subjected to a wide range of social attitudes in the Marines, plus being a member of the occupational forces of the Philippines and Okinawa, I came to believe the genesis of racism occurs during childhood.

If you were to place a black baby and a white baby side by side, they would play together without any problems. And if there were no other outside influences, they would grow up to realize that there were absolutely no differences between them *other* than the color of their skin—they have similar likes, dislikes, dreams, and desires.

The real problems begin when normally level-headed young men and women, black or white, fall under the spell of con men and people who have bigoted axes to grind. Whether these instigators are wearing white hoods or shouting "Black Power," they rely on mob-mentality to attain their goals. Because they are too cowardly to confront the alleged problem themselves, they rile up a mob to do their bidding. Once that happens, everything gets blown out of proportion, rational thought is devoured by hatred, and we find ourselves back at square one—every advance since the Emancipation Proclamation is wiped out.

Until mankind addresses the problems existing between the haves and the have-nots, hatred will continue to flourish. Of course, this has been civilization's most volatile issue since Cain sucker-punched Abel.

Living is based on relationships interwoven with common interests, goals, and the fulfillment of dreams. Life is about the pursuit of happiness, which certainly is made easier if you have respect for your fellow human beings regardless of race, religion, or gender. That's the message I received from my father, and it was the core of almost everything the Marines drilled into me. I learned that you can't buy respect; it must be earned. And the best way to earn it is by treating others as you would like to be treated. Do that and life isn't as difficult as we make it out to be.

I've never made a big deal about race in my personal or professional lives, yet people have just naturally assumed I have racial hang-ups because of my heritage. After all, aren't all southerners naturally semiliterate, slow-talking, slow-moving, gun-totin' rednecks who sing "Dixie" while pledging allegiance to the Lost Cause? As ridiculous as that analogy sounds, there are those who still perceive origin of birth as defining literacy, morals, politics, and religion.

When I first arrived at the University of Nevada-Reno, there was only one black kid on our boxing team. Whenever we went on the road to battle other universities, everyone would pair up for rooms and it always came down to me and this black kid being left to room together. But our coach Jimmie Olivas, figuring I had racial attitudes because I was from the South, had me room with him, and the black kid got a room all to his own.

When I went to work for the phone company in Reno after graduation, they sent me to San Francisco to be interviewed by one of the bigwigs from Pacific Bell. This gentleman glanced at my application and, noting that I was a southerner, said, "You know, we have a lot of colored people working for us."

I just looked at him and said, "So what?"

"Well, I just wanted to know if working for colored people would bother you," he said.

I said, "Sir, I was an enlisted man in the United States Marine Corps. My tent mate was a colored guy, which means we slept side by side, about as close as two men can get with it still being legal. So I don't understand what the big deal is about."

What I wanted to tell him but didn't, for an obvious reason, is that everyone is equal in the eyes of a Marine drill instructor. Everyone's a turd—a whale turd, to be exact. All of us were the lowest things at the bottom of the sea. There was no discrimination. It was no different from what Henry Jordan said it was like playing for the Green Bay Packers under Vince Lombardi: "Lombardi treated us all the same—like dogs."

All Marine boots, regardless of race or creed, were shitbirds. When one member of our platoon screwed up, everyone suffered. Endless push-ups and squat-thrusts, agonizing minutes holding an

M-1 at arms' length and scrubbing the deck with bristle brushes worked wonders when it came to getting seventy young men to get with the program. As such, each of us gradually put aside our animosities, our petty hatreds, and dislikes and became a team—a brotherhood in which the only color that was important to us was Marine green.

Racial hatred is for fools. Where would I be today if it hadn't been for Coston Donahue and Harold Williams, the two black Marine sergeants who taught me almost everything I know about boxing? Harold Williams was the greatest boxing coach I've ever had and when he was teaching me how to hook and throw the cross, the fact that he was black and I was white didn't mean a goddamned thing. Color never entered into the equation. He was willing to teach and I was willing to learn and together we made one helluva team. That's what the Corps is all about—accomplishing your mission through teamwork.

Don't get me wrong. Just because you're a Marine doesn't mean you can't be biased or a bigot. But if you can accept the *truth,* accept people for what they are and not focus on their color, then you have taken the first step toward becoming a righteous human being.

Of course, over the years I have seen my share of assholes, good ol' boys raised on nothing but hate and ignorance. But that war was fought and lost a long time ago, and I believe it's high time everyone got his or her head screwed on right.

One of my best friends in Nevada is Luther Mack, and I love the guy and think he is one of the greatest men I have ever met. Although Luther just happens to be black, what truly matters is that he's a good man. And he's also one of the most honest and trust-worthy people I've ever been around.

Luther also knows people and is a master at detecting bullshit. I remember one time Don King walked up to him and said, "How ya doing, brother." Luther replied, "I am *not* your brother. You can call me Mr. Mack or you can call me Commissioner Mack. But I am a member of the Nevada State Athletic Commission, which supervises boxing in this state. You are a promoter. I am not your brother."

Luther's a *Man,* and we see eye to eye on a lot of things, most of which center around one theme: He doesn't want people rubbing it in his face because he's black and I don't want people rubbing it in my face because I'm white.

In this same vein, I do not care for people who say "Because I'm a black person I am entitled to . . ." That's nonsense, because the *only* thing any of us are entitled to is equal treatment.

For example, Jesse Jackson is entitled to nothing more than I am and I'm entitled to nothing more than Luther Mack. Just because you happen to be black does not entitle you to anything special. Affirmative action is wrong because it perpetuates discord, distrust, and dislocation of the very principles this nation was founded upon. If we continue on this destructive path the axiom "I can be all that I want to be" will no longer hold true because it will require the politically correct addendum "Just as long as I am the proper color, proper gender, and balance the prescribed quota."

The way you make affirmative action work is by treating all children equally from the time they are born. Do that and you wipe out racism in one generation. What you can also do is strengthen the existing laws and make the penalties more severe for those individuals or corporations that do not treat everyone equally in the workplace. If you make the penalties exorbitant, sexual abuse and discriminate hiring practices would cease overnight.

I believe in fairness for everybody and if anyone—black or white—needs financial help, then you have a moral obligation to help him or her get through the rough times. I am more than willing to help anyone who is trying hard and wants to get it together. While that has nothing to do with race, it has everything to do with being a righteous human being.

In court there are instances where I have to fine someone and instruct him or her to make restitution. But I always tell them: "I don't expect you to pull a rabbit out of the hat. You can't do what you can't do, but I do expect you to try. And if you try, I'll work with you. But if you don't try, then I'll come down on you hard."

∞∞∞∞∞

While a lot of people have different beliefs about the relative intelligence of the various races, I believe that a person's intelligence has nothing at all to do with the color of his or her skin. It is my belief that you are born with certain tools as an individual and you have to commit to using those tools and working hard. If you do that you can be successful; if you don't you can fail. As Coach Lombardi once said, "Winning is a habit. Unfortunately, so is losing."

As such, whenever I hear someone in our courtroom ranting and raving about "I'm this or that because of two hundred years of slavery," or something of the like, I make it clear that I believe they are mistaken. I tell them:

> *You are what you are, because of what you have chosen to make of yourself. There is right and there is wrong, and the fact that you chose to follow the path of criminal behavior is your fault. And you can't lay it off on what happened years ago. To do so is an excuse, a parachute, a way to shirk responsibility.*
>
> *If that were the case then General Colin Powell would have never had the opportunity to fulfill his dreams. Because he just happened to be born with black skin, there would have been only one course for him to follow. According to your bullshit theory Powell would be on Death Row right now, instead of being honored as one of the greatest military heroes in our nation's history.*

Colin Powell and other great black men like him have succeeded and will continue to succeed in our armed forces because they were and still are *allowed* to do so, just as Hispanics, Asians, and Caucasians are *allowed* to do so. Nothing is given to you in the Army, Navy, Air Force, Marines, or Coast Guard; everything is earned. There are no quotas to be filled in regard to race or gender, and a man's or woman's worth is determined by individual talent, experience, and intelligence. And for that reason alone we have the greatest military force in the history of mankind.

But it wasn't always that way. When the question of desegregating our armed forces was first raised shortly after World War II, the majority objected to it. But when the plan was enacted in 1947 it succeeded beyond anyone's wildest imagination—because the penalty for disobeying was so severe. Justice has about as much to do with military justice as does music to military music. Disobey a direct order and you find yourself in the brig; neither the military court nor your military defense council cares about your family's social standing, your gender, or the color of your skin. Orders are orders, and if you should be unfortunate enough to have blatantly disobeyed one then you can kiss your butt good-bye.

Of course, there is such a power base of naysayers out there that the implementation of the military's approach to race and gender relations could never be achieved in the civilian world. These soulless bastards wring their hands and complain that "life is not fair" while brainwashing the masses into believing their twisted interpretation of equality—that of "rewarding the have-nots by penalizing the haves." For reasons that escape me, no one challenges this misguided concept and "we the people" continue to be imprisoned by the damnation of affirmative action and other divisive tools of ignorance.

As long as this nation rewards mediocrity and laziness—wasting its time in a futile search for excuses instead of searching for viable solutions—we will continue to stumble along a path that leads to doom.

We have perverted our so-called civil liberties to the point that we have irrevocably blurred the definitions of right and wrong. We are so concerned about the rights of criminals that we have lost sight of the rights of the victims. Black-on-black crime is epidemic and our educational system has become so fouled that teachers are now more concerned about their own safety than teaching their students the fundamentals of life. Our welfare system is nothing more than a sick joke played upon those less fortunate, both white and black, stripping away their self-reliance and their self-respect.

But little is done to correct these situations because "we the people" are so handcuffed by political correctness and our twisted concept of race relations that we allow ourselves to be chained within a dark, deep dungeon built upon the dictates of stupidity.

Progress, whether it is of a social or economic nature, is relative, and the majority always end up being dragged kicking and screaming into the modern age. Let's face it, the bulk of our civil rights laws would never have come about if it had been left up to popular vote.

As a district court judge I am often asked to preside over naturalization hearings. What I end up telling these new citizens is this: "As I stand here today, I look out and I see black people from Ethiopia, brown people from Mexico and Haiti, and I see men and women from the Orient and the Balkans. In a few moments you will be taking the oath of allegiance to the United States and you will become Americans.

"Some day in the future someone will ask you what nationality you are and it is my hope that you tell him or her that you are an *American*—not an African American, Hispanic American, Haitian American, or any such divisive term. It is my hope that all of you will now concentrate on what makes us equal instead of what makes us different. If you do this you will succeed beyond your wildest dreams."

While I believe there is absolutely nothing wrong with being proud of your heritage, I do not believe it is reason enough to warrant exceptional compensation. Being an American means you enjoy a freedom and an opportunity to succeed on your own terms. This is a luxury of democracy that is not enjoyed by those living under a reign of terror or in abject poverty in places like Angola, Zaire, El Salvador, or Mexico. As such, Africa is a good place to be *from*. The same can be said about Afghanistan, Yugoslavia, Russia, South and Central America, or any of the fractured nations of the Middle East.

There is a Chinese proverb that says: "To dwell on the past is to rob the present. But to forget the past is to rob the future." In essence, while remembrance can be a positive force as we attempt to avoid repeating yesterday's mistakes, it becomes a negative if guilt is continually laid at our neighbor's feet.

As a nation we must move forward, not backward. Our efforts are best served in quest of harmony, not animosity. Dwelling on hate and discord kills the soul while forgiveness nurtures tolerance, which replenishes vitality. It is the spirit of this nation, complete with its diversified people, that has held us together for the better part of two centuries—through a multitude of wars and fractured peace, through social distrust and fragile harmony. This vitality will persist only as long as we continue to pull together.

Instead of bitching about what we can't do, let us concentrate on what we can do. The inheritance we extend to future generations will surpass that which was passed on to us if we can put aside our petty jealousies, our gender discord, and our excuses that today's failures are the direct result of what happened a century and a half ago.

No matter how it is packaged, whether black or white, hatred and distrust are as insufferable as they are intolerable. We would be wise to heed the advice of José Martí, the brilliant Cuban patriot and scholar, who once said, "Mankind is composed of two sorts of men—those who love and create, and those who hate and destroy."

Only by directing our efforts on the former can we be truly blessed as a land of the free.

Family Matters

Although I do not play golf or tennis, I do enjoy a game or two of hold 'em poker. I still find time to run three miles four days a week and I keep my upper body in shape by working on the heavy and light bags. I cringe every time I see someone who is grossly overweight, and I am angered to the point of tears in the courtroom when I see those who are obviously guilty beat the rap because of a stupid mistake by a police officer or a prosecutor.

I believe in capital punishment and the undeniable right of law-abiding citizens to arm and defend themselves. I prefer jeans to dress trousers, own only one suit and two sport coats, and have worn the same tuxedo for the past fifteen years.

I have simple tastes, many dislikes, and a few people I love to death. I am hardheaded as well as baldheaded, yet uncomplicated to the point of simplicity. I have made as many mistakes as any five men I know, yet I still believe I'm the luckiest sonofabitch in the world.

As much as I love my darling sons and wife, I flat-out refuse to go on vacations with them. This is more for their benefit than mine. For example, the first and last time I went on a trip with my family was an excursion to Canada. As soon as we hit the border, this uniformed bureaucrat asked me why I was traveling to his country.

"Business," I told him.

"What kind of business, sir?" he replied.

"*Business* business," I said, thoroughly steamed. "And what the hell's it to you?"

Of course, Kaye and the boys started laughing, which did nothing to soften the situation with the border guard. Although we were allowed to travel throughout that beautiful land without too many people being insulted by my brash behavior, the point is that I'm just not good company away from the environment in which I feel most comfortable. I enjoy spending time with my family at home, I enjoy the atmosphere of the courtroom, and I feel at ease around boxing folk. Everything else is foreign.

But no matter where I am, my family is not far away.

In the right-hand drawer of the judge's bench upon which I reside are two power grips, one with "Tommy" written on it with a black ink marker and the other with "Terry" emblazoned on it in big, bold letters. Even when I'm wrapped up in a trial and am unable to hug my children as much as I would like, I will pull out those power grips and figuratively give my boys a big squeeze. And when I'm out of town refereeing a fight I will often take my sons with me. But even if I can't, they are never far from my mind.

I love my sons as much as I love life, and I make sure they know this each and every day. Children need to know what's in their parents' hearts. They have enough problems as it is without confusing them further.

Although I'm sure that my daddy was proud of me, he never verbalized it to me. And he never pulled me aside and told me he loved me.

In 1959, when I was discharged from the Marine Corps, I remember walking into the house and hugging my mother, then stepping back to greet my father. As expected, he was as formal as ever, sticking out his hand and expecting me to shake it, real gentlemanlike. Instead, I pushed his hand away and hugged him.

Later, one of my brothers told me my father had said, "Mills hugged me." I always hug Terry and Tommy.

Daddy was proud of me, yet he never shared those sentiments with me. He was set in his ways and couldn't change. He viewed life through the eyes of a farmer, and until the very end he couldn't understand why I chose to view things differently. During his last visit to Reno in 1982, I was driving him around and showing him the sights when he suddenly turned to me and said, "Son, I have never seen a place so unblessed by nature."

That's my father—hardheaded and set in his ways. He wanted me to walk in his footsteps, and when I chose a different path he refused to discuss the matter. But he was a good daddy, and I was lucky to have him.

On June 5, 1984, my brother Remer called me at six o'clock in the morning and told me that our father had died in his sleep at the age of seventy-four. I cried like a baby. But once I composed myself, I called back and told Mom I wanted to see him.

"You can't," she said. "He's been taken to the mortuary."

My father believed in organ donation and once that process was attended to, he was cremated before I had a chance to take one last look at him. My father's last wish was that there not be a big funeral, and only my mother, my brothers and sister, and my father's sister attended the graveside service at St. Bonaventure Cemetery in Savannah.

Once the service was concluded, we were standing around the grave looking at that little metal urn when one of the cemetery attendants politely told us it was time to close up the grave. I looked at him, feeling about as empty as a man can feel, and I said, "Give me that shovel."

I buried my daddy.

Regrets linger long past the grave, though. I can't help but wish my father were sitting here beside me right now so I could tell him just how proud I am of what he accomplished in life. And, hopefully, he could tell me the same.

More than anything, though, I would finally tell him how much I love him.

∞∞∞∞∞∞

I want my sons to be as happy as they can possibly be. Right now Terry has set a goal of attending Stanford University, which is great. I'll do everything in my power to make that dream come true. What I won't do is put undue pressure on my boys to do any certain thing. I want them to decide.

My primary goal in life is now my sons' happiness. When they reach maturity and it is time for them to take that big step into the real world, I want them to do something that is productive, something they can succeed at. But whatever they decide to do, as long as it isn't illegal, I'm going to say, "Sons, just do your best. That's all I ask. I am not going to try to live your life for you, so do what you've got to do. All I desire is your happiness. And if you attain that, then I will be the proudest father on the face of this earth."

I think it's wrong for a parent to plan out a child's life. The way I look at things is that each of us gets one shot and one shot only at making the most out of life. We are given a limited number of mental and physical tools plus the opportunity to expand our knowledge concerning the proper way to use these gifts. And then the curtain is raised and we walk out there upon life's stage and we perform.

While the actual performance is ours and ours alone, just how long we get to do so is out of our control.

∞∞∞∞∞

The boxing bug bit Terry in the summer of 1995, and Greg Rice, a good friend, started teaching him the finer points of the sweet science. He was such a quick study that I had absolutely no qualms about him taking his first amateur step during that year's Thanksgiving holiday. He was in good shape, overflowing with confidence, and was even properly dressed for the occasion. Eleanor Ennis, a friend of the family from Atlanta who had designed boxing outfits for several world champions, got Terry a pair of custom-made trunks.

But just before his amateur debut, Terry started having difficulty keeping food down. He was vomiting all the time and we suspected it was just a bad case of the flu. But when it persisted for almost a week, we took him to the doctor and he was diagnosed as having an unknown strain of sinus virus. The vomiting was so persistent that the only way to stop the reaction was with daily hypodermic injections. But what truly baffled the doctors was that Terry's bowels had completely shut down, and not even suppositories helped remedy the situation. His health deteriorated to the point where, on three separate occasions in a three-month span, we had to rush him to the hospital so that he could be fed intravenously.

Kaye and I have never felt so helpless in our lives. Our son was sick, real sick, yet no one could tell us why. Of course, Terry handled it better than we did. Only once can I remember him ever feeling sorry for himself. He was lying in bed one night and said, "Daddy, why is this happening to me?" And because I did not have an answer, all I could do was hug him and cry.

Every test and examination which could be done locally was done. Finally, we took Terry to Stanford University, where further tests were conducted. The university even assigned a special health care administrator to assure us that everything humanly possible was being done for our son. It was to no avail, because even the nation's top medical specialists were baffled. Everyone was so frustrated that finally one of the administrators told Kaye, "We don't like admitting this, but we do not know what's wrong with Terry.

This is beyond medical science. But we do believe that when his body is ready to get better, he *will* get better. If he doesn't, however, we will have to send him somewhere else. Where that will be, we do not know."

It got so bad that there were times that I could not keep my mind on the proceedings in my courtroom. All I could think about was Terry lying in bed, needles stuck into his arms and legs, and intravenous feeding tubes keeping him alive . . . *God, please please help me!*

Midway through one trial I was intent on the prosecuting attorney's presentation and then my mind just went blank. I felt the tears burning my eyes and all of a sudden I had this urge to write down my thoughts. I opened a drawer on the bench in search of a sheet of paper, but all that was in there was the cardboard backing of a legal pad. What I proceeded to write was straight from a broken heart—the words any loving father would write with his child at death's door:

"God—I hope Terry is okay. He is a good boy and doesn't deserve this. Let it be me. I will take it, but not Terry. I know I am not very deserving, but please let my son get well. I love my son. Lord, let him be okay."

I put that piece of cardboard back in the drawer, brushed aside my tears, and then tried to get my mind back on the trial. A few weeks later, Terry said, "Daddy, I have to go to the bathroom." Just like that, my son started to heal.

It's amazing the number of things we take for granted. For almost three months the first thing I asked Terry each evening was, "Have you had a bowel movement today?" For obvious reasons, taking a crap isn't something we give much thought to. Little do we realize that when our body ceases to rid itself of its refuse, it will kill us. And that's what was happening to my son.

But then Terry's body finally tired of the puzzling virus that was killing him and a miracle happened. That's the only way I can explain it.

It was almost a year later that I remembered that piece of cardboard in the drawer in the courtroom. When I started to read the anguish that I had recorded months earlier, tears once again filled my eyes. And that's when I picked up a pen and humbly wrote: *"Thank you, Lord. My boy got well. I'll try to be a better person."*

And, by God, I'm still trying.

∞∞∞∞∞

I love my wife, Kaye, every bit as much as I love our sons. Of course, she deserves at least one Medal of Honor for putting up with me over the past eighteen years. I can't say enough about Kaye. She is without doubt one of the greatest things that has ever happened to me.

Every marriage partner has his or her little quirks, and the way you make that marriage last is to work around these shortcomings. Of course, it took me quite a while to figure that out, having botched my first two trips to the altar.

During my senior year at the University of Nevada-Reno in 1963, I married Diane Rosse. But three months into the marriage, we realized our bond was infatuation, not love. Although we

divorced, we parted friends. Four years later, I met and fell in love
with Judy Miller, who had a son, John, through a previous marriage. We married, I adopted John, and we had a daughter, Marilyn,
who was born in 1972. By this time I was working in the district
attorney's office and became immersed in the job, working week-
ends and seldom devoting time to my family. It proved to be a dis-
astrous mistake on my part, because Judy sued for divorce in 1974.
The blame is mine and mine alone.

But every once in a while you get lucky, and God gives you a
gift. Little did I know that when Bob Perry, a Reno lawyer friend
of mine, stopped by to visit one night in 1979, I would eventually
end up with three such gifts. Although I was dating, the last thing
on my mind was marriage. I was thirty-seven, had plenty of money
in my pocket, an apartment, and had learned how to operate the
washing machine and microwave oven. Life was good.

And then Bob talked me into having a beer with him at the
Hardy House in downtown Reno. Some female juvenile probation
officers eventually joined us, and we shared stories about our
respective jobs. When the subject reverted to dating, a pretty young
lady named Kaye Pearce pointed at me and said, "That guy right
there would be too short for me."

My response: "Well, fuck you."

Instead of being offended by my coarse comeback, Kaye
laughed. In short order we began dating, eventually were married
in 1980, and have shared our laughter ever since. Of course, we laid
out the ground rules beforehand. She knew that I am consumed by
my job, referee prizefights as a hobby, and am hardheaded and
highly opinionated. She also knew that I was head over heels in
love with her.

So we tied the knot. Very tightly, in fact. I am convinced that if you practice at something long enough, you eventually get it right. Kaye is everything a man could ask for. She has beauty and brains, temperament and tolerance. She has given life to our two darling sons, Terry and Tommy, and they, in turn, have greatly enhanced my life. Kaye is as good a soulmate as I could ever desire. We see eye to eye, and heart to heart. She knows my pressure points as well as I know hers, and we work like hell to avoid needlessly upsetting each other.

More than anything else, though, I allow Kaye to be her own person and she reciprocates. She doesn't bitch when I play poker, and I don't bitch when she goes shopping.

I love Kaye as fervently as any man can love a woman. And when I step into a prizefight ring, even though I am not allowed to wear jewelry because it might come in contact with one of the fighters and thus cause injury, my wedding ring is carefully tied to the laces of my right shoe. I do this because I want to, not because it's fashionable.

I suspect that you cannot be a good daddy, a good husband, or a good person unless you are happy with yourself. If you are doing something you dislike or do not believe in, whether it is a job or a marriage or whatever, then you are going to be one miserable sonofabitch. It's easy to be personable and outgoing if you're happy with yourself. But if you find yourself in a situation that is like being in prison—you're boxed in by four unbending walls and the only door leading to freedom is locked—then you might as well fold your cards and leave the game.

The bottom line is I like being married to Kaye, and in no way, shape, or form does our relationship resemble anything close to being a house of detention. I am not in this relationship against my will. The choice was mine. The same can be said of the duties of being a father, refereeing prizefights, and working as a district court judge. Dammit, I love life and I wouldn't trade mine for anything.

Granted, I am a bit odd. For instance, my definition of "ecstasy" is a card game such as that which I sat in on a while back in Las Vegas. The concept of "Bad-Beat Jackpot" poker is that the guy that does the beating gets 30 percent of the pot, the guy that gets beat gets 40 percent, and the table shares the other 30 percent.

In this instance, the cards were dealt and I had the king-ten of spades as my hole cards. The gentleman sitting directly across the table from me had pocket aces, but he didn't know how to play poker worth a damn. He bet, I raised, and instead of raising and running me off the hand, he stood pat and called. The ace of spades, jack of spades, and the jack of hearts popped up on the flop. Of course, because neither of us knew what each other's hole cards were, I had no way of knowing he was in the driver's seat with aces-full and he had no way of knowing I was looking for the biggest damn draw card of them all. Nonetheless, he bet and I raised and once again he called instead of raising me back.

So help me God the last flop card was the queen of spades. I had my royal flush and all I wanted to do was jump out of my chair and dance around the casino. Instead, I kept my game face as the other guy opened the betting. I raised the bet and said, "Sir, I hold the stone-cold nut."

"You've got four jacks?" he replied.

I grinned at him and said, "No sir. I have *the* stone-cold nut—a royal flush."

Damn, that was the greatest feeling in the world. Because it was "bad-beat," the guy with the aces-full won $2,600 to my $1,400. But if he had raised the bet on the first flop I would have ended up with nothing because I would have folded my hand.

My point is that sometimes you have to make the right call, go for the best hand, even if it costs you.

It's simply amazing to me, though, how so many people are unable to grasp this concept. If you hold on to a mere handful of guidelines—being honest with others and yourself, treating your fellow men and women as you would wish to be treated, plus having the personal integrity to do what is right instead of what is fashionable—then you've got the world by the short hairs. I'm sure there is some complicated highbrow word for behaving in this manner, but for the sake of argument I prefer to call it being "tough, but fair."

I have a very special leather belt buckle and I only wear it when I referee a prizefight. The buckle is hand-tooled and into it is carved two boxing gloves, two prizefight rings, and my name and initials. The buckle was made in a prison leather workshop and came to me one day in the mail from Lyndon Kelso, who was serving life without parole. I had prosecuted Lyndon years earlier for a triple homicide, but it was a crime that did not insult me. A murderer who kills during a burglary or a rape, or in the course of child abuse, or a mob hit, I don't care if they put that sonofabitch *under* the jail. But Lyndon's case was much different.

He had been married to a good woman, but at age sixty-five he got stupid and left his wife in order to shack up with another woman who wasn't so good. Lyndon ended up being played for a fool because he spent all of his money on this not-so-good woman, and once he was broke she started sleeping around with someone else. He was sitting in the living room of his trailer home late one night and feeling like an idiot when she walked in with a big satisfied smile on her face.

"Well, you spent all night with him again, didn't you?" Lyndon said.

"That's right," she said, "and I'm still sore in the crotch, so what are you going to do about it?" Lyndon responded by shooting her twice and then went over to where this other guy lived and shot him dead. This guy's thirty-three-year-old son just happened to be there, so Lyndon shot and killed him, too.

There are *murders* and then there are murders. Lyndon Kelso simply got caught up in a crime of passion.

I'll never forget the letter that accompanied the arrival of the belt buckle: "Mr. Lane," Lyndon wrote, "what I did was wrong. But even though you convicted me of murder, you never once looked down your nose at me. You always treated me with respect during that trial. You treated me like a man. You were tough, but fair."

Fifteen years later I testified on Lyndon's behalf before the pardon's board. He was eighty at the time and had been diagnosed with cancer. I testified because I believe you can only punish someone so much.

Lyndon did eventually obtain his release, and I'm glad he did.

ROUND 12

Parting Shots

Bitching about problems accom-plishes nothing unless you have the stones to present some viable solutions. If you've followed me this far, you're well aware that my biggest hang-ups are the judicial system, the disintegration of the family, and the dubious state of professional boxing.

So let's get it on and do some more nut cutting. And a perfect place to start would be the fiasco that was the O. J. Simpson trial.

It is no big secret that prosecutors and defense attorneys will do everything within their power to take control of the trial, and in this instance the defense succeeded. Although Judge Lance Ito was pretty good on law, he lost control on the Friday before the trial actually began when Johnnie Cochran, Robert Shapiro, F. Lee Bailey, and Barry Scheck filed thirty-six defense motions.

If I had been the presiding judge, I would have told the defense team, "Gentlemen, this trial begins when I say it's going to begin. I told you this case would have opening statements at nine o'clock tomorrow, so your motions are all denied. If you have to make a record to protect your client, make them as we go along."

And when the two sides started those pissing matches, I would have recessed the jury and then called Gil Garcetti, the Los Angeles district attorney, and said, "I want you and every one of your deputies who plans to speak at this trial in my office in half an hour." I would have called Johnnie Cochran and told him the same thing. And when everyone was assembled, I would have said, "Okay, fuck with me if you want to, but if you do you have a serious chance of landing in jail."

Unfortunately, Judge Ito lost control of the trial and the lawyers ran the courtroom. For example, Barry Scheck's examination of Mr. Dennis Fung, the LAPD criminalist, was unnecessarily rude and so overbearing as to border on being criminal. I would have told Mr. Scheck, "Take the edge off your voice, the chip off your shoulder, and ask pertinent, nonrepetitive, legitimate questions or I'm going to get into your pocket."

Another inflammatory aspect of Scheck's interrogation of Mr. Fung is that *nobody* has seven days of evidence to impart. Yet Scheck labored and belabored the issues, dissecting Mr. Fung's every thought, thus boring the jury to death. All it would have taken me was five minutes of this nonsense and I would have called him to the bench and said, "Get to the point, dammit, and quit using a hammer on the poor bastard."

The bottom line is that the O.J. trial was a disgrace to anyone who has spent any time at all in a courtroom. Opening and closing arguments consumed four days each, yet the verdict was reached in less than four hours. The defense called 54 witnesses to the prosecution's 72. The prosecution spent 99 days presenting its case and the defense used 34 days in rebuttal. The jurors were sequestered 266 days in a three-ring circus of a trial that cost Los Angeles County $9 million. All this to have a verdict in less than four hours. I doubt the evidence was thoroughly reviewed.

I'm a firm believer in the truism that "All that's needed for evil to flourish is for good men to do nothing." It is time for the law-abiding citizens of these United States to demand that we judges take control of our courtrooms. To hell with the warm and fuzzy segment of society that decrees that criminals should not be held accountable for their crimes because they came from broken families or were abused as a child. We must demand accountability and require that our trials be a search for the truth.

The law is the law and it applies to both rich and poor, Californians as well as those from Vermont. A judge's duty is to preside, not play God. And if he or she refuses to appropriately carry this judicial burden, then it is our constitutional right to remove them from the bench.

Of course, the same can be said of boxing's more despicable characters.

∞∞∞∞∞∞

While prizefighting is a dirty and bloody business, there are quite a few honorable individuals in the profession. I've already mentioned Luther Mack and Marc Ratner of the Nevada State Athletic Commission as two of the most trustworthy people I have ever been associated with. Their integrity and honesty are impeccable. Suffice it to say that there are many more people, too numerous to mention, who are good and honorable, people whom I respect.

At the same time, though, the good are overshadowed by the bad. Until prizefighting can rid itself of the unmerciful flesh merchants, boxing will be perceived as a raft of bats and snakes.

While there is no way to eradicate the implications of organized crime, giant steps could be taken in this country to police the profession. For example, if all states established a high standard of regulation concerning legitimate licensing and medical procedures, such as those currently in place in Nevada, it would greatly reduce needless injuries.

One of the major problems existing today is that there are no boxing commissions whatsoever in many states. As such, a fighter can be knocked out in such a state on a Monday and climb back through the ring ropes on Wednesday in another, which is bullshit because it's evidence that the fighter's safety is being disregarded.

The only way prizefighting is going to earn legitimacy is to have basic standards and have those standards respected and enforced. It will take strong commissions and maybe if individual states will not deal with the problems, federal control, in the form of a boxing czar or something like that.

Those obvious problems aside, boxing could go a long way toward eliminating the physiological deterioration that causes all of the brain injuries by requiring fighters to maintain their respective weights. When I fought professionally, if you fought at eight o'clock that night then you made weight at noon that day. In my case, I would get off the scale and I would eat some eggs, juice, honey, and toast. I would take a nap and get up at four o'clock and eat my prefight meal, which was a steak. Today they say that's bad for you, so the fighters eat chicken and pasta. If I were fighting at 147, then I'd enter the ring at 149. I entered the weigh-in in shape and at the proper weight, and I climbed into the ring in shape and at the proper weight.

The way it's done now, though, the weigh-in is held the night before and the fighter eats a couple of times that night, goes to bed, wakes up, eats three more meals, and then fights. When Pernell Whitaker fought Oscar De La Hoya, Whitaker weighed 146 at the weigh-in and 159 at fight time. The last time I refereed a fight featuring Iran Barkley, he showed up at training camp weighing 211 pounds and had just a short time to dry out to the 168-pound limit. Barkley was a accident waiting to happen.

I'm not a doctor, but have you ever heard of a heavyweight dying of subdural hematoma? I haven't, because the fighters that die under those conditions are always the little guys, featherweights and lightweights. Their handlers dry these poor kids out, starve them until they can make the weight, and then pump them full of water and food after the weigh-in under the erroneous impression that they are rebuilding their man's physical strength. What these people are really doing is setting that fighter up for some type of injury predicated on improper management of weight.

If you're going to fight at the welterweight limit of 147 pounds, then you should weigh close to that at fight time. That is nothing more than being honest with yourself. More important, you are taking a major step in protecting your long-term well-being. What amazes me is why the trainers who have the real welterweights, the real lightweights, and the real middleweights don't stand up and say, "I don't give a damn what your rule is, sanctioning body. If my guy is going to fight at eight o'clock, then the guy he's fighting is going to be on the scales at noon that same day. And if he can't make weight, then he forfeits the purse and my man is the winner." Unfortunately the sanctioning bodies seem to be in the driver's seat on this issue.

The way it is done now is downright criminal.

We'll lop off the head of this snake by giving you a lethal quiz. What would you call a trainer who drastically dries out his fighter in order for him to make weight, watches from the safety of ringside as that young man fights and subsequently gets pummeled because he's too weak to defend himself, and then suddenly topples to the canvas, lapses into a coma, and dies the next day from a subdural hematoma?

I would call him an accessory to murder.

∞∞∞∞∞

One of the prosecutors who worked in the D.A.'s office when I was the district attorney thought of himself not only as a real hotshot lawyer but also a ladies man, and he made no secret of the fact that he was screwing around on his wife. When it came time for me to evaluate my staff and make promotions and award pay raises, this guy stepped into my office and said, "I understand that you don't appreciate how I'm conducting my private life."

I said "Let me tell you something. As long as you work here I am entitled to only two things: your loyalty and your diligence. I'm not entitled to your political support—I have to earn that. But I'm letting you know up-front that if you cheat on your wife, you cheat on me. You take vows. If you don't respect them, then how can I trust you?"

Well, that ol' boy didn't know what the hell to say. I guess he had become so enamored with himself and that artificial world he tinkered around in that he never stopped to think of the consequences of his actions. But then again, most people don't. They are so busy cutting corners and robbing themselves by shortchanging others that they fail to see the irreparable harm they inflict upon their fellow men, women, and children.

Of course, nothing you or I can say will straighten out these people. They have to do it themselves, and this happens only when their legs are knocked out from under them and they suddenly find themselves on the ground looking up. Sadly enough, I see far too many of these people in the courtroom.

It's a pathetic sight: Once successful businessmen who, either to support a mistress or cocaine habit, have gotten caught with their hand in the company till; mothers who have neglected their children for one unexplainable reason or another; and children from broken or fractured homes and from no homes at all. You look into their faces and see the hopelessness of what they've made of their lives, and you're sickened because someone has failed them along the way. Sadly enough, more often than not the culprits are the parents.

Parents tend to forget that children possess the greatest bullshit detectors of all time and they seem to see through our lies and half-truths quicker than do most adults.

Not only are kids not dumb, but they also tend to follow the most prevalent examples. It does no good to tell my children not to use drugs if the wife and I are smoking dope or popping pills for fun and relaxation. It does no good to tell my children that they must respect the opposite sex if I'm slapping my wife around every time she pisses me off, or if I'm sleeping around on her. It does no good to preach the value of honesty to my children if I'm bragging about how I ripped off the boss at work or how I pulled a fast one on the IRS.

Raise a child in an environment void of morals and you get an immoral child. But if you smother that child with love in an environment overflowing with kindness and goodwill, then the odds are in favor of that child doing likewise when he or she embarks on the tumultuous voyage of marriage and parenthood.

The bottom line is that we owe it to our children to do a better job of managing ourselves. And once that is accomplished, the residual benefit is better-behaved children.

The worst thing that happened to me as a child was when my father said he was ashamed of me. That was a whole lot worse than getting a belt applied to my butt. And so it is with my children. If I tell them I'm ashamed of them, they know damned well that they've screwed up pretty bad.

But that only works if you have set high standards for yourself and your children. Admonishing your child by saying "You could have done better than that" does little good if he or she sees you sloughing off at home or hears you bragging about how you're getting forty hours pay but doing only thirty hours of work on the job. You have to be careful of the messages you send to your children. They can't be proud of themselves if they aren't proud of mom and dad. And if that child isn't, then you've got trouble in the making— the sort of trouble I see on a regular basis in the courtroom.

I carry a snub-nosed .38 police special wherever I go, and if someone were to try to rob me or assault my wife I would put a slug between his or her eyes quicker than you can say "Miranda who?" That would be an instance when homicide is justifiable.

My point is that far too often I'll have a teenager brought to trial for breaking into someone's house intent on burglary and I'll tell him or her, "So far you have been lucky. But if you continue with this sort of behavior, one of these days you're going to break into the wrong house or apartment and someone is going to put a bullet in your brain and we won't have to worry about you anymore. I want you to think about that."

Hopefully they do, which allows us to avoid the terrible reality of having to bury another teenager who slipped out of his or her parents' grasp.

I wish there were simple answers to make it easier on today's parents. Other than policing ourselves and leading by example, the best advice I can offer is trying your damnedest to understand the pressures your children are going through. You do this by sitting down with them and really listening to them. Allow them to get things off their chest. You don't have to be their buddy, but you can lend them a sympathetic ear. You can let them know you honestly care about them and the burdens they are trying to shoulder.

Kids are not stupid and they know damned well that parents make mistakes. But they receive positive reinforcement when they see that you don't make the same mistakes over and over. Seeing is believing, and in no place is this any more important than in the home.

If you walk the walk at all times in front of your children—being honest and trustworthy, loyal and faithful, showing respect to others and demanding the same in return—then you've gone a long way toward pointing your kids down the right path.

It doesn't matter if you're wealthy or poor or come from a single-parent home. If you lack the basic disciplines, then you can't expect your kids to learn them by osmosis.

∞∞∞∞∞

We live in the greatest country in the world, yet we must remember that all great civilizations have been destroyed from within. We have something like one twenty-fifth of the world's population, yet we consume almost half of the world's food supply.

We have so much, and we waste so much.

We have to recognize that we can no longer hold ourselves above the rest of mankind. Not only do we have to start doing a better job of utilizing our natural resources, but we also have to start doing a better job utilizing our human resources. We have to do a better job of protecting what we've got, and the only way we can do this is by taking care of business. And this begins with taking care of yourself. Shape up and start developing a stronger moral fiber—stop the lies, put a halt to the half-truths, be honest with yourself and others. If your parents weren't strong, then become a strong parent anyway and don't wallow in the blame game. Work on improving your marriage instead of looking for the quickest and easiest way to bail out of it. Love your children as you were once loved. Take a moment to recall the fact that you were once as confused and susceptible to being led astray as are your children. What got you through those tough times is exactly what your own child needs right now—understanding and affection.

Despite what a small fraction of society believes, there is absolutely nothing wrong with the precepts of discipline, courage, persistence, teamwork, pride, loyalty, and brotherhood or sisterhood. Giving in to political pressure, political correctness, or any other form of political nonsense is to become a sheep being led to life's slaughter.

Instead, I prefer to survive. And the only way you truly succeed in that endeavor is by standing up for what's morally right regardless of the consequences. Put less emphasis on the selfishness of *I* and concentrate more on the unity of *we* and you will be truly amazed how smoothly a family can function. Do the right thing consistently day in and day out and you won't have any trouble looking at yourself in a mirror. Do this long enough and you'll be surprised how easily the good things in life start dropping into your lap.

It was a wise man who once said: "I don't care how much you know, I want to know how much you care." As such, I place more importance on what's inside an individual's heart than what's inside his or her bank account. Of course, while money doesn't buy happiness and being broke doesn't buy you shit, I would prefer the company of a poor yet honest man or woman to that of a morally bankrupt Wall Street banker.

We live in the age of excuses, which is no cause for rejoicing. I'm so sick and tired of people blaming their wives or their kids, their

231

secretaries or their bosses for their own failures. If everyone would start with the proposition that they are responsible if something goes wrong, then this world would be in a helluva lot better shape.

Of course, such an admission requires a great deal of personal integrity—the greatest of all human qualities, which far too often seems to be in short supply.

When I was a district attorney there was this eighty-year-old black gentleman who was arrested for carrying a concealed weapon—a derringer in his belt—while he was walking on Lake Street in Reno, a street once infested with whores and pimps and drug dealers. When he took the stand, I asked him, "Sir, why did you have that gun in your belt?"

And the old man just looked at me and smiled and said, "Mr. Lane, I'd rather you catch me with it than have them other folk catch me without it." I dismissed the case right then and there.

That's exactly how I feel about personal integrity. I believe what I believe, and there's nothing you can do to alter my stance. You can laugh at me, mock me, or knock me all you want about my being old-fashioned when it comes to morals and everything else I stand for.

But my bottom line is I'd rather be ridiculed for holding these ideals close to my heart than have the unethical bastards of the world catch me without them.

Postfight Reflections

I've always said there are three things I will not do: I will not wear platform shoes; I will not wear a three-piece suit; and I will not wear a toupee. I might as well add a fourth thing: I will not take up too much more of your time.

I'd be remiss in not thanking you for your patience. After all, I remember what it was once like to be young and energetic and how I'd start squirming and getting all fidgety whenever those old farts would ramble on and on and . . . well, obviously you know what I'm talking about. I think I've pretty much covered it all—my family, the Marine Corps, my daddy, life in and out of the prizefight ring, my trials and tribulations, my successes, and my many failures.

Because no one can go through life without the help of many good people, I hope I haven't omitted anyone who's lent a steady hand along the way. If I have, please allow me to admit wrongdoing right now and offer my apologies. It certainly wasn't intentional. Just blame it on the sluggishness of an old boxer's befuddled mind. Whoops, sorry—that sounds too much like an excuse, and I'm not in the excuse-making business. After all, I am what I am. And most of what I am right now is busy beyond belief. All because Mike Tyson bit a chunk out of Evander Holyfield's ear.

Right now, the schedule's hectic and every day's a new adventure. It seems as if there's always another new city to visit and new friends to meet. I've been to Boise, Kansas City, Savannah, and Augusta in the last two weeks alone. And in the process, I've met mayors and senators, club boxers and up-and-coming pros. I've even given speeches to groups of doctors and lawyers and whatnot.

In fact, I stunned a group of gentlemen not too long ago when I told them I didn't believe in the word *addiction*. Of course, everyone gasped. But they managed to catch their breath once I explained myself. My view of life, I told them, is that perseverance—getting your ears back and getting it done—is a habit. Unfortunately, so is quitting. And when someone comes into the courtroom and says, "Yes, Judge, I'm a thief. But it's because I have this drug problem," I tell him, "Son, the problem isn't drugs; the problem is you."

Let's say that you have a problem with booze and you go to a doctor and he or she tells you that you're an alcoholic. In the abstract, if you buy into the word *addiction,* that gives you an excuse for doing everything that's a product of addiction, whether it's beating your wife or becoming a thief to support that craving. Once you accept the premise of addiction, you've accepted an excuse for losing. And once you've done that—believing the proposition that drugs or booze is bigger than you are—then you've set yourself up for failure. When you buy into the idea that the problem isn't your fault, that it's the fault of the booze or the narcotics, then you're whipped. You're tossing in the gloves without a fight, which is bullshit.

Of course, while my views tend to be a bit controversial, I'm not about to put aside my beliefs simply because they might be interpreted as being offensive to those asking the questions. Everything considered, the inquisitors have been very fair and no one's taken a cheap shot at me. Believe me when I say I'm thankful, because it hasn't been for a lack of opportunity. I've been interviewed by all the top sports magazines and major metropolitan newspapers. *People* magazine did a nice piece on me and, of all things, *Esquire* listed me among "The 100 Best People in the World," which was really neat because I was right up there with Madeleine Albright, Willie Nelson, Christiane Amanpour, Muhammad Ali, the Dalai Lama, and, of course, Homer Simpson.

To quote Beverly Newell, my administrative assistant, "It's been hilarious."

Bev's a great gal, and I'd be lost without her. And I mean that literally and figuratively. It was her idea to set up the extra telephone lines at the office the day after Tyson's culinary gaffe. But even with five extra lines, we didn't have enough hours in the day to respond to all the interview requests. To quote Bev again, "The phones were ringing from daylight to dark. And when we weren't answering the telephone, we were trying to avoid all the cables and television cameras that seemed to be everywhere. It was absolutely crazy."

Even so, I've tried my best to be accommodating. The way I look at it, if someone is kind enough to ask my opinion, then I'd be a damned fool to turn him or her away. Besides, I've met some pretty nice people throughout this ordeal. And it's not as if this is manual labor. I mean, it's been fun. I've been interviewed on the radio by what seems like every station on the planet. I've refereed fights in parking lots of grocery stores, gymnasiums, and real ritzy casinos. I even refereed an arm-wrestling match in Ohio.

What's really blown me away, though, is people requesting my autograph. It's incredible. But as long as they are polite, I'm more than willing to sign. The only time I get irate by this signing business is when I hear of some hotshot baseball player who's making $3 million a year charging some ten-year-old kid $20 for an autograph. Know what that is? It's criminal.

By God, if you want my autograph, then you've got it—at no cost, my friend. And believe me when I say the honor is mine and mine alone.

But what's truly scary is that my so-called fifteen minutes of fame is like the Energizer Bunny—it just keeps going and going. Don't get me wrong, I'm not complaining. And neither is my wife. In fact, she's standing over my shoulder right now, bugging me about tracking down Mike Tyson's address. Why? "Because I want to thank him for making all this possible," Kaye says.

Come to think of it, maybe we should also extend our gratitude to Don King. After all, if he hadn't put up the stink about Mitch Halpern being the referee, I wouldn't be sitting here right now trying to compile my thoughts. By God, sometimes you receive help from where you least expect it.

Of course, what's kept me from getting too giddy or too full of myself is that I realize nothing is forever. I know this sucker is going to level off pretty soon, and then I'll be in for the big fall. So I'm planning for the future. There's a lot more coming up: a television show called *Judge Mills Lane—Justice You Can Trust,* like those other court dramas you see on TV. Also I'll be doing more speaking engagements. Plus working at a law firm in Reno, doing more private investigative work than defending criminals. But, knowing me (as you now do) you know I wouldn't defend a lot of the bastards out there anyway. Fanfare doesn't mean I've abandoned my principles. Some crimes still offend the hell out of me, and even if some damned rapist or murderer walked in with a wheelbarrow full of money, I'd toss his ass out the door.

And this brings up the obvious question: How much longer will I referee? I honestly don't know. Not too long ago I made the mistake of saying I'd walk away at sixty. But now . . . well, I just can't put a year on it. As everybody knows, nature is a great equalizer—you don't hear the bell quite as well or move quite as fast. I've also seen a lot of folks who have just stuck around too damned long. I'm not about to make the same mistake. When I can't do it the way it's supposed to be done, then I'm gone. Because I'm still in pretty good shape, I imagine I'll be up there in the ring for a few more years. I'm not looking beyond that. When the time does come to pack it in, I'll pack it in. Until then, I'll give it my best shot. As always.

I reckon this is as good a place as any to take off the gloves and call a halt to this literary fight. Honest to God, squaring off against Mike Tyson has to be a helluva lot easier than mastering the mysteries of syntax. I just hope I haven't put on a miserable performance.

Before I go, though, I'd like to leave you with one last picture. I'm standing on the back deck of a nice fashionable home in a nice fashionable neighborhood, peering through the darkness of a pleasant star-filled summer evening, past the valley that extends down to the city lights of Reno far away. And what I'm thinking right now is that my daddy was right when he told me that I would never truly be happy unless I made my own way. And now that that's the case, I've come to the realization that I have been really lucky because all things are now shared, the most important of which is my love for my wife, Kaye, and our darling sons, Terry and Tommy. What bears repeating is that I consider myself to be the luckiest sonofabitch on the face of the earth. I've had more good times than anyone should be allowed to have in a lifetime. I love life, I love boxing, and I love my job at the courthouse and the people I work with. But most of all I love my family. And I'm excited about the future.

And right now, as my eyes adjust to the darkness, and the glittering casino lights of downtown Reno come into focus, I bow my head in thanks for a truly wonderful yesterday and today, and all the promises of an even better tomorrow. All things considered, I might not have been a champion but I sure as hell was a pretty damned good contender. And it's been a "kick in the ass" along the way which is why I'm breathing real easy at the moment, filling my lungs with this good high desert Nevada night air and smiling like a little kid at Christmas.

I'm smiling because I am quite at peace with the past and present. In fact, life has a rather unique fragrance to it at the moment, because a soft wind just carried to me the sweet scent of alfalfa and cowshit. And it smells good, damn good.

∞∞∞∞∞∞

Mills Lane retired from the bench May 1, 1998, and is now engaged in the active practice of law in Reno, Nevada, for Lane, Fahrendorf, Viloria, and Oliphant.

MILLS LANE'S TOP TEN FIGHTS

1. Danny "Little Red" Lopez vs. Salvadore Sanchez, June 21, 1980, Las Vegas, Nevada, for the WBC featherweight championship.

"Little Red" has always been one of my favorite fighters. He wasn't very colorful and he didn't have great talent, but he had great heart and great courage. It was said of him: "The best thing about 'Little Red' is the way he left his opponent. On the floor." On the other hand, Sanchez was a magnificent fighter. And in this bout, he hit Lopez with a left hook and a right uppercut midway through the fourteenth round. I immediately stepped between them and saw that "Little Red" had no idea what was going on. I stopped the fight and told him, "I'm sorry, Danny, but it's time." Sanchez was later killed in an automobile accident. Had that not happened, I believe he would have gone into the history books as one of the great featherweight champs of all time—every bit as good as Willie Pep and Sandy Sadler.

2. Ken Norton vs. Larry Holmes, June 9, 1978, Las Vegas, Nevada, for the WBC heavyweight championship.

After a seven-year hiatus, I was assigned this fight despite the protests of Jose Sulaiman, president of the WBC, and Don King. Sulaiman was still upset about the Maracaibo, Venezuela, fight in which someone at ringside altered my scorecard. Because of the lingering controversy about my qualifications, I put a lot of pressure on myself. Moments before the fight I remember thinking, "Man, this is for the heavyweight championship of the world. Don't make any mistakes." I didn't. And for the most part, neither did either fighter. In fact, Holmes won the early rounds and Norton came back to win the middle and late rounds. The fight was almost dead even going into the fifteenth, and Holmes got the best of that round to win the title. Before the fight he said that he'd take a swim in the Caesars Palace pool if he won. And sure enough, he did exactly that, which delayed the postfight press conference.

3. Evander Holyfield vs. Riddick Bowe II, November 6, 1993, Las Vegas, Nevada, for the WBA-IBF heavyweight championship.

Of course, this was the bout in which the idiot "paraglider" dropped in on us. That insanity aside, this fight had as much brutal nonstop action as any I've ever refereed. As always, Evander was in tip-top shape. Bowe, however, hadn't attended to business and wasn't at his best. He did give it his all, and I don't believe there was a lull in the fighting. What was truly remarkable about Holyfield, though, was that not once did he back away from Bowe, no matter how hard the champ hammered on him. The action was so fast and furious that both guys continued beating on each other after the bell ending Round 12. Although it certainly wasn't intentional, Bowe nailed me with a good shot to the back of the head as I stepped between the fighters to break it up. Evander won on a decision, regaining the title he had lost to Bowe a year earlier.

4. Marvin Hagler vs. John Mugabi, March 10, 1986, Las Vegas, Nevada, for the world middleweight championship.

It started raining just before the fight began and then it turned chilly. The fight was held in an outdoor arena at Caesars Palace, and I remember looking over at Hagler in his corner and saw steam rising from his bald head. With the imminent threat of more rain, vendors were selling garbage bags for $10 at ringside. Hagler was one of the most complete packages I've ever seen. He was a natural left-hander with a good right hook, but he could switch to a right-handed style with no problem. Mugabi was also a tough customer, and he could knock you dead with one shot. He wasn't big as middleweights go, but he gave Hagler all he could handle. Mugabi kept the fight close in the early rounds, but then Hagler started nailing him with a left-handed lead and kept the pressure on. Mugabi almost went down in both the ninth and tenth rounds, but somehow held on. Then, in the eleventh, Hagler clobbered him with eight or nine straight punches and Mugabi went down for good.

5. Michael Carbajal vs. Humberto Chiquita Gonzalez, March 13, 1993, Las Vegas, Nevada, for the IBF-WBC light flyweight championship.

Novice fight fans think that the heavier the fighters, the better the fight. For my money, I'll take two good flyweights any day. In this instance, everyone knew that Carbajal was a tough kid, but no one really knew what was inside his heart. Gonzalez, on the other hand, was well known as a big puncher. Early in the fight Carbajal got knocked down, but was back up on his feet in no time. It wasn't a devastating punch, but Carbajal knew he'd been hit. And then, I believe it was in the fifth round, Carbajal got knocked down again. This time, his leg twisted under his body, and when they go down like that they don't normally get back up. But by the time the count reached seven, Carbajal started up and was on his feet by the count of eight. I remember Gonzalez looking on in amazement. It was as if Gonzalez was saying, "Damn, I took my best shot at him and I can't put him away." After that, it was a war and Carbajal ended up knocking out Gonzalez in the seventh round. From start to finish, both fighters battled like true champions, and the crowd certainly got its money's worth.

6. Mike Tyson vs. Evander Holyfield II, June 28, 1997, Las Vegas, Nevada, for the WBA heavyweight championship.

Tyson's reason for disregarding protocol and taking a bite out of Evander's ear in the third round was that he'd been head-butted by Holyfield earlier in the bout. Of course, the head-butt wasn't intentional. In fact, you can expect that to happen whenever these two

guys get together. Tyson's style is to lower his head and wade in;
Evander's style is to stay on top of you and not give an inch.
Therefore the clash of skulls was inevitable. In fact, I would have
indicted Holyfield for stupidity if he'd tried to avoid bumping heads
with Tyson. I know I've said this before, but it does bear repeating:
Holyfield pounded Tyson unmercifully through the first two
rounds, and wasn't fazed in the least by Tyson's best shots. Bite or
no bite, Evander Holyfield was far and away the best fighter in the
ring that night. Tyson's third-round disqualification saved his body
a lot of wear and tear.

   7. Evander Holyfield vs. Carlos DeLeon, April 9, 1988, Las
      Vegas, Nevada, for the WBA-WBC-IBF cruiserweight cham-
      pionship.

Years from now everyone is going to be studying Holyfield's fights,
trying to document when he threw his best right hand, left hook,
and so on. It's kind of comical really, because for so long everyone
ignored him. After all, Evander's critics said, he might have been
the greatest of all cruiserweights, but he was just an undersized
heavyweight. Surely he was no match for Mike Tyson and the other
so-called big guys. I've never felt this way because I saw him at his
absolute best, albeit as a 195-pound cruiserweight against DeLeon.
What everyone loses sight of is that Rocky Marciano, one of the
two or three greatest heavyweights of all time, only weighed in at
186 pounds. And Joe Louis, another of the top three heavyweights,
fought at 199 pounds. The bottom line is that Holyfield, whether
he's at 195 or 212, is a champion's champion. DeLeon was no
slouch, yet Holyfield gave him such a beating that I had to stop the

fight in the eighth round. He flat-out tore DeLeon apart, and that's saying an awful lot about any prizefight.

8. Donald Curry vs. Milton McCrory, December 6, 1985, Las Vegas, Nevada, for the WBA-WBC welterweight championship.

The action was light through the first two rounds, but Curry hit McCrory with a tremendous right early in the third round and McCrory went down. When he got up, I could see that his legs weren't that steady. But because it was a title fight, I elected to allow him to continue. I waved both fighters to resume the action, and again Curry unloaded with another tremendous right hand— *splat!* Honest to God, McCrory went down as if someone had shot him and I counted him out. I've always thought that if Curry had taken care of himself, if he'd kept in shape and attended to business, he might have gone into the record books as one of the greatest welterweights of all time. Of course, this never happened. He was a classic example of an athlete who abused his tools. But on this night, Donald Curry was every bit as good as Marvin Hagler.

9. Livingston Bramble vs. Ray "Boom Boom" Mancini, February 16, 1985, Reno, Nevada, for the WBA lightweight championship.

This was a classic example of two totally different lifestyles in action. On one side of the ring was Mancini, a kid with great character but not a lot of natural talent. His father was a highly regarded lightweight before World War II, and on this night "Boom Boom" dedicated the fight to his dad, who was at ringside. On the other side of the ring was Bramble, as weird a person as I've ever known in boxing. Bramble was a dreadlocked Rastafarian from the Virgin Islands. No matter where he went he brought his pets with him—a boa constrictor, an alligator, and a pit bull. On this night he was one of the greatest fighters I've ever seen. Of course, Mancini was no slouch either. In fact, neither fighter backed away; they stayed on top of each other throughout the entire fifteen rounds. Bramble had the upper hand, committing no tactical errors, and hit Mancini no less than 255 times square in the face. As such, he was awarded a well-deserved unanimous decision.

10. Bert Cooper vs. Evander Holyfield, November 23, 1991, Atlanta, Georgia, for the WBA-IBF heavyweight championship.

The videotape of this fight should be seen by anyone who is trying to put his or her troubles behind them. The message conveyed by both fighters is simple: No matter how hard outside forces are trying to belittle you, if you believe in yourself and your abilities, then no power on earth can stop you. Cooper was ridiculed by the media to no end, yet when he entered the ring he rose above the nonsense and showed everyone exactly what was inside his heart. Whenever I run across someone who is going through difficulty, I tell them: "If you can reach deep down into yourself and extract one-tenth of what Bert Cooper did against Evander Holyfield, then you'll become a champion. Maybe not a boxing champion, but a champion of the human race." I realize I've belabored the point, but both Cooper and Holyfield's gutsy performances in this fight is really what this book is all about—getting knocked down, but getting back up on your feet; taking the hard knocks, but continuing to battle on because you refuse to quit on yourself.

WORLD CHAMPIONSHIP FIGHTS
REFEREED BY MILLS LANE

1. November 20, 1971
    Betulio Gonzalez D15 Erbito
    Salavarria, WBC flyweight;
    Maracaibo, Venezuela

2. June 9, 1978
    Larry Holmes W15 Ken Norton,
    WBC heavyweight; Las Vegas,
    Nevada

3. June 3, 1979
    Lupe Pintor W15 Carlos Zarate,
    WBC bantamweight; Las Vegas,
    Nevada

4. November 30, 1979
    Vito Antuofermo D15 Marvin
    Hagler, world middleweight;
    Las Vegas, Nevada

5. June 21, 1980
    Salvadore Sanchez TKO14
    Danny Lopez, WBC feather-
    weight; Las Vegas, Nevada

6. October 2, 1980
    Saoul Mamby W15 Maurice

Watkins, WBC junior middleweight; Las Vegas, Nevada

7. April 11, 1981
    Larry Holmes W15 Trevor
    Berbick, WBC heavyweight;
    Las Vegas, Nevada

8. June 27, 1981
    Aaron Pryor TKO2 Lennox
    Blackmore, WBA junior welter-
    weight; Las Vegas, Nevada

9. August 10, 1981
    Antonio Avelar KO2 Tae-Shik
    Kim, WBC flyweight; Seoul,
    Korea

10. December 5, 1981
    Art Frias KO8 Claude Noel, WBA
    lightweight; Las Vegas, Nevada

11. February 15, 1982
    Sugar Ray Leonard TKO3
    Bruce Finch, world welterweight;
    Reno, Nevada

12. June 11, 1982
    Larry Holmes TKO13 Gerry
    Cooney, WBC heavyweight;
    Las Vegas, Nevada

13. May 20, 1983
    Larry Holmes W12 Tim
    Witherspoon, WBC heavyweight;
    Las Vegas, Nevada

14. November 25, 1983
    Larry Holmes TKO1 Marvis
    Frazier, WBC heavyweight;
    Las Vegas, Nevada

15. March 9, 1984
    Tim Witherspoon W12
    Greg Page, WBC heavyweight;
    Las Vegas, Nevada

16. February 16, 1985
    Livingstone Bramble W15
    Ray Mancini, WBA lightweight;
    Reno, Nevada

17. May 20, 1985
    Larry Holmes W15 Carl
    Williams, IBF heavyweight;
    Reno, Nevada

18. August 10, 1985
    Hector Camacho W12 José
    Luis Ramirez, WBC lightweight;
    Las Vegas, Nevada

19. December 6, 1985
    Donald Curry KO2 Milton
    McCrory, WBA-WBC welter-
    weight; Las Vegas, Nevada

20. March 10, 1986
    Marvin Hagler KO11

John Mugabi, world mid-
dleweight; Las Vegas, Nevada

21. March 23, 1986
    Dwight Braxton TKO6 Leon
    Spinks, WBA cruiserweight;
    Reno, Nevada

22. April 19, 1986
    Michael Spinks W15 Larry
    Holmes, IBF heavyweight;
    Las Vegas, Nevada

23. November 22, 1986
    Mike Tyson TKO2 Trevor
    Berbick, WBC heavyweight; Las
    Vegas, Nevada

24. March 7, 1987
    Mike Tyson W12 James
    Bonecrusher Smith, WBA-WBC
    heavyweight; Las Vegas, Nevada

25. May 30, 1987
    Tony Tucker TKO10 James
    Douglas, IBF heavyweight;
    Las Vegas, Nevada

26. August 1, 1987
    Mike Tyson W12 Tony Tucker,
    WBA-IBF-WBC heavyweight;
    Las Vegas, Nevada

27. October 29, 1987
    Thomas Hearns KO4 Juan
    Roldan, WBC middleweight;
    Las Vegas, Nevada

28. November 21, 1987
    Julian Jackson TKO3 Chul Baek,
    WBA junior middleweight; Las
    Vegas, Nevada

29. April 9, 1988
Evander Holyfield TKO8 Carlos
DeLeon, WBA-WBC-IBF cruiser-
weight; Las Vegas, Nevada

30. April 16, 1988
Mark Breland D12 Marlon
Starling, WBA welterweight; Las
Vegas, Nevada

31. June 6, 1988
Virgil Hill W12 Ramzi Hassan,
WBA light heavyweight; Las
Vegas, Nevada

32. July 28, 1988
Michael Nunn TKO9 Frank Tate,
IBF middleweight; Las Vegas,
Nevada

33. October 29, 1988
Raul Perez W12 Miguel Lora,
WBC super bantamweight; Las
Vegas, Nevada

34. November 4, 1988
Thomas Hearns W12 James
Kinchen, WBO supermid-
dleweight; Las Vegas, Nevada

35. November 7, 1988
Roger Mayweather W12 Vinny
Pazienza, WBC junior welter-
weight; Las Vegas, Nevada

36. February 4, 1989
Marlon Starling TKO9 Lloyd
Honeyghan, WBC welterweight;
Las Vegas, Nevada

37. February 25, 1989
Julian Jackson KO8 Francisco De

Jesus, WBA junior middleweight;
Las Vegas, Nevada

38. March 6, 1989
Hector Camacho W12 Ray
Mancini, WBO junior welter-
weight; Las Vegas, Nevada

39. December 9, 1989
Jorge Paez TKO6 Lupe Gutierrez,
IBF featherweight; Reno, Nevada

40. April 14, 1990
Michael Nunn W12 Marlon
Starling, IBF middleweight; Las
Vegas, Nevada

41. May 19, 1990
Pernell Whitaker W12 Azumah
Nelson, WBC-IBF lightweight;
Las Vegas, Nevada

42. July 8, 1990
Aaron Davis KO9 Mark Breland,
WBA welterweight; Reno,
Nevada

43. August 11, 1990
Pernell Whitaker KO1 Juan
Nazario, WBA-WBC-IBF light-
weight; Lake Tahoe, Nevada

44. August 19, 1990
Maurice Blocker W12 Marlon
Starling, WBC welterweight;
Reno, Nevada

45. October 25, 1990
Evander Holyfield KO3 James
Buster Douglas, WBA-WBC-IBF
heavyweight; Las Vegas, Nevada

46. February 23, 1991
Pernell Whitaker W12 Anthony
Jones, WBA-WBC-IBF light-
weight; Las Vegas, Nevada

47. March 18, 1991
Simon Brown TKO10 Maurice
Blocker, WBC-IBF welterweight;
Las Vegas, Nevada

48. June 3, 1991
Thomas Hearns W12 Virgil Hill,
WBA light heavyweight;
Las Vegas, Nevada

49. July 12, 1991
Tony Lopez TKO6 Lupe
Guttierrez, IBF junior light-
weight; Stateline, Nevada

50. September 14, 1991
Julian Jackson KO1 Dennis
Milton, WBC middleweight;
Las Vegas, Nevada

51. October 5, 1991
Pernell Whitaker W12 Jorge Paez,
WBA-WBC-IBF lightweight;
Reno, Nevada

52. November 23, 1991
Evander Holyfield TKO7 Bert
Cooper, WBA-IBF heavyweight;
Atlanta, Georgia

53. November 29, 1991
James McGirt W12 Simon
Brown, WBC welterweight;
Las Vegas, Nevada

54. December 7, 1991
Rafael Pineda KO8 Roger

Mayweather, IBF junior welterweight; Reno, Nevada

55. February 15, 1992
Julian Jackson TKO1 Ismael
Negron, WBC middleweight;
Las Vegas, Nevada

56. March 20, 1992
Iran Barkley W12 Thomas
Hearns, WBA light heavyweight;
Las Vegas, Nevada

57. April 11, 1992
James Toney W12 Glenn Wolfe,
IBF middleweight; Las Vegas,
Nevada

58. May 9, 1992
Terry Norris TKO4 Meldrick
Taylor, WBC junior middle-
weight; Las Vegas, Nevada

59. June 19, 1992
Evander Holyfield W12 Larry
Holmes, WBA-WBC-IBF heavy-
weight; Las Vegas, Nevada

60. August 1, 1992
Julio Chavez TKO4 Frankie
Mitchell, WBC junior welter-
weight; Las Vegas, Nevada

61. September 12, 1992
Michael Nunn W12 Victor
Cordoba, WBA supermiddle-
weight; Las Vegas, Nevada

62. March 13, 1993
Michael Carbajal KO7 Humberto
Chiquita Gonzalez, IBF-WBC
light flyweight; Las Vegas, Nevada

63. May 8, 1993
Gerald McClellan TKO5 Julian
Jackson, WBC middleweight;
Las Vegas, Nevada

64. June 7, 1993
Tommy Morrison W12 George
Foreman, WBO heavyweight;
Las Vegas, Nevada

65. November 6, 1993
Evander Holyfield W12 Riddick
Bowe, WBA-IBF heavyweight;
Las Vegas, Nevada

66. February 19, 1994
Humberto Chiquita Gonzalez
W12 Michael Carbajal, WBC-IBF
junior flyweight; Ingelwood,
California

67. March 4, 1994
Gianfranco Rosi TD6 Vincent
Pettway, IBF junior middleweight;
Las Vegas, Nevada

68. April 9, 1994
Tracy Patterson W12 Richard
Duran, WBC junior feather-
weight; Reno, Nevada

69. April 22, 1994
Michael Moorer W12 Evander
Holyfield, WBA-IBF heavy-
weight; Las Vegas, Nevada

70. May 7, 1994
Julio Cesar Chavez W12 Frankie
Randall, WBC junior welter-
weight; Las Vegas, Nevada

71. July 2, 1994
John Avila TKO12 Stanley
Longstreet, IBO welterweight;
Lake Tahoe, Nevada

72. September 17, 1994
Julio Cesar Chavez TKO8
Meldrick Taylor, WBC junior
welterweight; Las Vegas, Nevada

73. January 28, 1995
Rafael Ruelas TKO8 Bill Schwer,
IBF lightweight; Las Vegas,
Nevada

74. February 18, 1995
Oscar De La Hoya W12 John-
John Molina, WBO lightweight;
Las Vegas, Nevada

75. April 8, 1995
Bruce Seldon TKO7 Tony Tucker,
WBA heavyweight; Las Vegas,
Nevada

76. May 6, 1995
Johnny Tapia TD8 Ricardo
Vargas, WBO junior ban-
tamweight; Las Vegas, Nevada

77. June 17, 1995
Riddick Bowe KO6 Jorge Luis
Gonzalez, WBO heavyweight;
Las Vegas, Nevada

78. July 9, 1995
Tracy Patterson TKO2
Eddie Hopson, IBF lightweight;
Reno, Nevada

79. July 15, 1995
Orlando Canizales W12

John Lewus, IBC junior featherweight; Stateline, Nevada

80. September 9, 1995
James Toney WDQ5 Earnest
Mateen, WBU light heavyweight;
Las Vegas, Nevada

81. September 16, 1995
Julio Cesar Chavez W12 David
Kamau, WBC junior welter-
weight; Las Vegas, Nevada

82. November 28, 1995
Vernon Forrest W12 Marlon
Thomas, IBC junior welterweight;
Augusta, Georgia

83. March 16, 1996
Mike Tyson TKO3 Frank Bruno,
WBC heavyweight; Las Vegas,
Nevada

84. June 1, 1996
Alberto Jimenez W12 Jose Lopez,
WBO junior bantamweight;
Lake Tahoe, Nevada

85. August 4, 1996
Michael Clark W12 Mauro
Lucero, IBC lightweight;
Columbus, Ohio

86. September 7, 1996
Terry Norris TKO5 Alex Rios,
IBF-WBC junior middleweight;
Las Vegas, Nevada

87. November 9, 1996
Michael Moorer TKO12

Frans Botha, IBF heavyweight;
Las Vegas, Nevada

88. December 6, 1996
Montell Griffin W12 James
Toney, WBU light heavyweight;
Reno, Nevada

89. January 18, 1997
Oscar De La Hoya W12 Miguel
Angel Gonzalez, WBC junior
welterweight; Las Vegas, Nevada

90. February 7, 1997
Lennox Lewis TKO5 Oliver
McCall, WBC heavyweight;
Las Vegas, Nevada

91. April 12, 1997
Oscar De La Hoya W12 Pernell
Whitaker, WBC welterweight;
Las Vegas, Nevada

92. April 18, 1997
Junior Jones W12 Marco Berrera,
WBO junior featherweight;
Las Vegas, Nevada

93. June 28, 1997
Evander Holyfield WDQ3
Mike Tyson, WBA heavyweight;
Las Vegas, Nevada

94. July 12, 1997
Lennox Lewis WDQ5 Henry
Akinwande, WBC heavyweight;
Stateline, Nevada

95. August 3, 1997
José Rivera TKO6 Rocky

Gannon, IBA light heavyweight;
Columbus, Ohio

96. October 7, 1997
    Bronco McCart W12 Eric
    Holland, IBA junior middleweight;
    Auburn Hills, Michigan

97. October 14, 1997
    Saul Montana W12 Kenny Keene,
    IBA cruiserweight; Boise, Idaho

Fight certification: Ralph W. Citro, Inc. Mr. Citro is the current director of IBRO, the International Boxing Research Organization.

INDEX

I N D E X

262